ENGLISH FOR THE GLOBAL AGE WITH CNN VOL.20

Kansai University CNN Research Group

ASAHI PRESS

《《《 音声ストリーミング配信 》》》

http://text.asahipress.com/free/english/

この教科書の音声は、
上記ウェブサイトにて無料で配信しています。

English for the Global Age with CNN, Vol.20
Copyright © 2019 by Asahi Shuppan-sha
All rights reserved. No part of this publication may be reproduced in any form without written permission from the authors and the publisher.

は　し　が　き

　本書は 2000 年から出版されている English for the Global Age with CNN International シリーズの 2019 年度版です。この 1 年間に起こった出来事の中から、日本人の英語学習者の関心を呼んだトピックを選び出しました。

　経済状況が低迷するなか、わが国は大地震、津波、また豪雨など、未曾有の自然災害に見舞われ、さらに原発事故の後遺症が尾を引き、国の将来像がますます見えにくくなっています。そのような状況のもと、英語に対するニーズは相変わらず高いものがあります。社内の共通言語として英語を導入した大手企業の出現が、すでに 10 年余り前のこと。その後、さらにいくつかの大企業が英語重視の方針を採っていることは周知のことかと思われます。ただ、背景の事情は微妙に変化しつつあります。これまでのように、日本の若者が英語を身につければ社会で活躍する場がある程度保証されるわけではなく、むしろその前段階として、海外からの優秀な人材との競争に生き残るために最低限必要とされる能力として、高い英語力が求められているのです。そのようになってくると、本当に私たちに要求されているのは、英語で世間話ができたり、資格試験の成績を高めるということだけではないでしょう。むしろ、時々刻々と変化する世界情勢を的確に把握し、異なる意見をもつ人たちと対等に渡り合える英語力、またそれを裏打ちする教養こそが重要になってきます。そのような意味において、24 時間体制で世界のニュースを発信し続ける CNN の放送を利用することは、私たちの英語運用能力を高めるばかりか、物事を考えるときの大きな糧 (food for thought) になるといっても過言ではないでしょう。

　本書の編集方針は、今を考える上で注目したいトピックに対して、リスニング、ライティング、ボキャブラリーの問題を配することによって、重要な表現が身につくよう工夫してあります。また、世界各地からのレポートを聞くことによって、グローバル時代の英語 (Englishes) を体験してもらえるよう編纂しました。各レッスンの作業内容を以下に記しますので、その趣旨を十分に理解された上で、本書を最大限に活用してください。また、教室内における本書の使用と併行して、朝日出版社から月刊で出ている CNN の情報誌 English Express を利用することも、運用能力の更なる向上にたいへん役立つと思われます。

Warm up

レッスンに出てくるニュースの一部を取り上げて、「聴き取り」と「内容理解」のポイントを解説しています。ウォーミングアップとして練習して、本篇への準備をしてください。

Words and Phrases to Study

レッスンに現れる重要な語彙を取り上げました。Definitions のセクションで、定義に該当する語彙を上の語群から選んでください。また、それぞれの語（句）を Examples にあげた例文の適切な場所に必要があれば変化形にしたうえで、入れてください。

Blanks to Fill In

ここでは、指示にしたがって、ストーリーを聴き取ってください。空所には 1 語ずつ単語が入ります。聴き取りは、この教科書の中心的な作業です。納得のいくまで、何度も繰り返し聴くことが大切です。

Judgments to Make

ストーリーを聴いた上で、このセクションの英文が内容に合致しているかどうかを考えてください。もし合致していれば T、違っていれば F で答えます。F の場合、正しい英文に直して言ってみましょう。

Partial Composition

ストーリーに現われた表現を使って、日本文を英語に直してみましょう。一見難しそうですが、Blanks to Fill In をよく見直して、使えそうな表現を探し出してください。

なお、最後になりましたが、本書編集の段階で、朝日出版社の日比野忠氏をはじめ、英語テキスト編集部の皆さんには、前編以上にお世話になりました。この場をかりて御礼申し上げます。

2018 年 10 月　関西大学 CNN 英語研究会

奥田　隆一
カイト由利子
山本　英一
A. S. Gibbs
A. Bennett
Oliver Belarga
北村　裕

Contents

はしがき
CNNニュースの特徴 ii
CNNで話される英語の特徴と音声変化のポイント vii

Unit 1: **Well Suited for Royalty** 1
　　　　英王室、新時代！　ハリー王子とメーガンさん婚約

Unit 2: **Never More Timely** 10
　　　　ノーベル平和賞にICAN 核兵器禁止条約の採択に貢献

Unit 3: **Miracle Transformer** 19
　　　　チャーチルそっくりの特殊メイクで辻一弘氏、アカデミー賞受賞

Unit 4: **Lukewarm Welcome** 28
　　　　昨年の認定はわずか28人　難民に門戸を閉ざす均質社会日本

Unit 5: **Otherworldly Genius** 37
　　　　車椅子の天才物理学者逝く　ホーキング博士からのメッセージ

Unit 6: **A Different London Tube** 46
　　　　ロンドン地下の旧「郵便鉄道」が新たな観光路線として復活

Unit 7: **Where France Meets Arabia** 55
　　　　ダ・ヴィンチの傑作を展示　ルーブル・アブダビついに開館

Unit 8: **Storing It and Sharing It** 64
　　　　電力の約80%を再エネで賄う！　独の住宅用蓄電池システム

Unit 9: **Dutch Ingenuity** 73
　　　　国土の約4分の1が海面下　オランダが世界に誇る洪水対策

Unit 10: **Putin's Soft Spot** 82
　　　　実は無類の動物好き！　こわもてプーチンの懐柔法

Unit 11: **Neither One nor the Other** 91
　　　　返還から20年　中国の統制強化 vs. 民主化要求で分断する香港

Unit 12: **Giant Smog Trap** 100
　　　　中国の大気汚染を救う？　スモッグを"食べる"巨大空気清浄機

CNN ニュース英語の特徴

　ニュースと言えば、新聞やインターネットで読める「書かれた記事」と、ラジオやテレビやインターネットなどで聴取できる「音声や画像による記事」がある。新聞英語に関しては独特のスタイルがある。また、テレビやラジオのニュースにもある程度スタイルがある。定時のニュースではアナウンサーが書かれた記事を読むので、スタンダードな英語が話される。しかし、テレビでは特に現場でのインタビューなどがそのまま放送されることが多い。CNN ニュースの特徴は、現場からのレポートが、ほとんどの場合そのまま採用されていることである。ここに、書かれた新聞英語と語られる放送英語の特徴の違いが出てくる。以下では、CNN ニュースでよく耳にする現場からのレポート中心の英語の特徴をまとめておくことにする。

1　CNN ニュースの特徴

　CNN ニュースでは、アンカーが原稿を読み上げるのではなく、話題について短く述べ、次に現地のレポーターの報告を放映するという形式が取られている。また、インタビューがそのまま使われているので、インタビューを受けた人の準備なしの受け答えの口語英語の特徴が頻繁に見られる。

2　口語英語の特徴

特徴 1：あらかじめ準備された英語でないので、考えながら話すということがあったりするため、文の途中でポーズがおかれたり、意味のない表現が挿入されたり、文構造が途中で変わったりする。

(1) well とか you know, you see, kind of, say という表現の多用
(2) 同じ単語や表現の繰り返し
(3) 文の途中の無音のポーズ
(4) 日本語の「えー」とか「あのー」にあたる意味のない erm という語が使われる
(5) 文構造が途中で変わってしまう

特徴 2：省略や縮約形が多用される。

(6) I'm や You've などの縮約形や短縮形の使用：

I am → I'm, I would → I'd, they are → they're, do not → don't, have not → haven't, are not → aren't, were not → weren't, does not → doesn't, has not → hasn't, was not → wasn't, did not → didn't, had not → hadn't, should have → should've, because → cos

(7) 接続詞の that や目的格の関係代名詞の省略：

I think (that) he is a good man.

(8) 文頭の省略：

I hope he's coming. → Hope he's coming.
Do you want a drink? → Want a drink?
You/We'd better be careful. → Better be careful.
That sounds nice to me. → Sounds nice to me.

特徴3：等位接続詞と付加疑問文の多用

(9) 等位接続詞の多用：従位接続詞や分詞構文を使うとより堅苦しくなるので、口語英語では等位接続詞の and, or, so などが文頭で多用される。
(10) 付加疑問文の多用：アンカーとレポーターのやり取りで確認をする時によく使われる。

<例1>
You type, he records. (8)**Doesn't** even matter if he can't see the screen.

<例2>
We just (1)**kind of call** (6)**'em** his shoes. "Come put your shoes on.".

<例3>
When I saw him sprinting like that, it was amazing. (2)**It…it** just… (5)**I couldn't** believe it.

<例4>
People want to use… (5)**people have** their mobile phones. And it's a great, we think, new addition to have these green boxes around London.

<例5>
Sherry Portanova: (1)**Well**, at first, he really does not want you to put (6)**'em** on there. But once he has them on, then (6)**he's** just happy as a clam to go out and run around.

<例6>
Japan needs more women to have children. The fertility (6)**rate's** low; the population (2)**is…is** getting older and shrinking; but this stagnant

economy also needs more workers—a double crisis facing lawmakers.

＜例7＞

Matthew Chance: (2) **Do...do** you think, one day, it could become more important to Russia than, say, Europe?
Lilya Ivanova (Student of Mandarin): I (6) **don't** think that it will be more important (2) **in...in** culture, but in business, I think (7) **it** will be so.

＜例8＞

Waheguru Pal Singh Sidhu (Brookings India): People have used the phrase *frenemies*. I would actually reverse that and say this is more like enefriends. (1) **You know,** (9) **so,** (6) **it's** more that they were thought of as enemies but (6) **they're** trying to see how they can be friends.

＜例9＞

Nina dos Santos: (9) **So**, my average day starts at around about five thirty in the morning. I'll often have sent off a couple of e-mails, probably from bed; tapped away silently … (4) **erm** … before six a.m. (9) **And** then I make my way into the office around about seven, seven thirty. Then I'll head into makeup. (6) **I'll** check my e-mails when I get to my computer, read through the rundown, then (6) **it's** into the studio.

3 CNNの決まり文句

(A) CNNのニュースではレポーターが登場するが、「…については〜がお送りします。〜さん！」とアンカーが呼びかける。この時には次のような表現が使われる。

(1) Here's 〜. という表現

<u>Here's CNN's Kyung Lah</u> with the story.

(2) 〜 explains という表現

<u>Jim Boulden explains</u>.

(3) 〜 looks at ... という表現

Sumnima Udas now <u>looks at</u> the changing relationship between Beijing and New Delhi.

(4) ~ have a look at ... という表現

World affairs correspondent Jill Dougherty <u>has a look at</u> a very familiar face and name.

(5) ~ takes a look という表現

<u>John Vause takes a look</u> from Beijing.

(6) ~ reports on ... という表現

and <u>Liz Neisloss reports on</u> the training that leaders say will sharpen the country's competitive edge and boost the bottom line.

(7) ~ file a report という表現

And CNN's Neil Curry <u>filed this report</u> from the "blue carpet."

(8) ~ spoke to ... という表現 ＜インタビューをしたという事を述べている＞

<u>Paula Hancocks spoke to</u> some of the workers at Fukushima.

(9) ~ brings us ... という表現

<u>Our Ralitsa Vassileva brings us</u> an amazing story of faith, survival and love.

(10) ~ gives us a lesson という表現

<u>CNN's John Vause gives us a lesson</u>.

(11) ~ shows us ... という表現

For this week's Eco Solutions, <u>Kyung Lah shows us</u> how the recent nuclear crisis could fuel a shift in where Japan gets in energy.

(12) ~ has the story. という表現

Lisa Sylvester <u>has the story</u>.

(13) ~ has the details. という表現

<u>Samuel Burke has the details</u>.

(14) As ~ explains, ... という表現

<u>As David McKenzie explains</u>, adults can now face stiff fines or even jail time if they don't call Mom and Dad.

(15) As ~ reports, ... という表現

<u>As Will Ripley reports</u>, an eruption would be disastrous.

v

(B) レポートの締めくくりの表現

レポートの最後には「…から〜がお伝えしました」と言う。この場合には、「レポーターの名前＋所属＋現地名」という形式が使われる。現地名がそんなに有名でない時には、(2) のように、国名もその後につけられる。もちろん所属は CNN なので、「レポーターの名前，CNN，現地名」となる。また (3) のように、現地名ではなく場所の名が使われたり、(4) のように番組名が使われたりもする。(5) の例のように現地名が省略されることもある。

(1) Sumnima Udas, CNN, New Delhi.
　　(CNN のスムニマ・ウダスがニューデリーからお伝えしました)

(2) Will Ripley, CNN, Mount Fuji, Japan.
　　(CNN のウィル・リプリーが日本の富士山からお伝えしました)

(3) Jill Dougherty, CNN, the State Department.
　　(CNN のジル・ドーティが国務省からお伝えしました)

(4) Laurie Segall, CNN Money, New York.
　　(CNN マネーのローリー・シーガルがニューヨークからお伝えしました)

(5) Ralitsa Vassileva, CNN.
　　(CNN のラリッツァ・バシルバがお伝えしました)

CNN で話される英語の特徴と音声変化のポイント

1. CNN で話される英語の特徴

　一つのトピックの中で、アンカーがアメリカ人でレポーターがイギリス人、またはその反対ということが普通なので、アメリカ英語とイギリス英語の両方が使われるのが CNN の英語の特徴だ。どのアンカーとレポーターがアメリカ英語を話し、どのアンカーとレポーターがイギリス英語を話すのかをあらかじめ知っておくと、各英語の特徴がはっきり分かって、聴く時の参考になる。以下に、各アンカーとレポーターの話す英語を中心に分類し、各英語の特徴のまとめを示し、具体例をあげて解説する。さらに、オーストラリア英語とカナダ英語のアンカー、レポーターもあげておいた。また、英語を聴き取る時のポイントになる音声変化についても具体例を挙げて解説しておいたので、参考にしていただきたい。

1.1. アメリカ英語の発音の主な特徴

[特徴 1] /æ/ という発音

　まず、アメリカ英語で一番の特徴というのは、/æ/ という発音だ。日本語の「ア」の口の構えで「エ」を発音した音に近い。c<u>a</u>t, f<u>a</u>t, m<u>a</u>d, J<u>a</u>pan 等の語の下線部の音。

[特徴 2] /t/ や /d/ という音の弾音化

　その次に特徴的なのは、/t/ や /d/ という音が、弾音化して /r/ に近い音になることだ。computer は「コンピューラー」に、better は「ベラー」に、powder は「パウラー」に、louder は「ラウラー」に、water は「ワーラー」に、party が「パーリー」に聞こえる。

[特徴 3] /ər/ /əːr/ という発音

　さらに、アメリカ英語で特徴的なのは、/əːr/ という発音だ。口をあまり開かず「アー」と「ウー」の中間のような音に近い。語尾に現れる /ər/ と語中に現れる /əːr/ だが、この /r/ の発音はイギリス英語では使われない事に注意。pap<u>er</u>, met<u>er</u>, keep<u>er</u> などや l<u>ear</u>n, c<u>er</u>tain, <u>ear</u>th などの語の下線部の音。

[特徴 4] /ɑ/ という発音

　もう一つの特徴は、イギリス英語では /ɔ/ と発音するところで、/ɑ/ と発音することだ。h<u>o</u>t, g<u>o</u>d, w<u>a</u>nt 等の語の下線部の音。「ア」の口の構えで「オ」を発音したような音。イギリス英語の方は唇を少し丸めて発音される。

1.2. アメリカ英語を使う主なアンカーとレポーター

Kristie Lu Stout
10代からモデルとしても活動。スタンフォード大学においてメディア研究で学士号と修士を取得。北京の清華大学で中国語も研究。現在はCNN Internationalのニュースストリームのアンカーを務めている。

1-02

Kristie Lu Stout: Now, living (1) <u>near</u> (a) <u>an active</u> volcano would seem to be a dangerous choice, but more than 13 million people (b) <u>have made</u> their home in Tokyo, just two hours' drive from Mount Fuji. As Will Ripley reports, (c) <u>an eruption</u> would be (2) <u>disastrous</u>.

【アメリカ英語の発音の特徴】

(1) near ▶ /ər/ という発音。[特徴3]
(2) disastrous ▶ /æ/ という発音。[特徴1]

【音声変化のポイント】

(a) an active ▶ an の /n/ と active の語頭の /a/ がつながり「アナクティブ」と聞こえる。
(b) have made ▶ have の /v/ が /f/ と弱音化され、後の made の /m/ とつながり「ハッメイド」と聞こえる。
(c) an eruption ▶ an の語尾の /n/ と eruption の語頭の /ɪ/ がつながり「アネラプション」と聞こえる。

Will Ripley
CNNの東京支局の特派員として活躍中。ジャーナリストとして15年の経験を持ち、日本からアジア太平洋地域に及ぶ主要なニュースを担当。コロンビアのミズーリ大学でジャーナリズムを学び、ベテランのカメラマンや編集者としても活躍している。

1-03

Will Ripley: (1) <u>Patrick</u> Schwarzenegger, (a) <u>son of</u> the world-famous (2) <u>Terminator</u>, is posting pictures (b) <u>of his</u> (1) <u>Japanese</u> (1) <u>vacation</u>: posing with a sumo wrestler; visiting the Meiji Shrine; eating (3) <u>lots of sushi</u>.

【アメリカ英語の発音の特徴】

(1) Patrick, Japanese, vacation ▶ /æ/ という発音。[特徴1]
(2) Terminator ▶ /r/ という発音。[特徴3]
(3) lots ▶ /ɑ/ という発音。[特徴4]

【音声変化のポイント】

(a) son of ▶ son の語尾の /n/ と of の /ə/ がつながり「サノブ」と聞こえる。
(b) of his ▶ of の語尾の /v/ と his が /iz/ と弱形で発音され、つながって「オブイズ」と聞こえる。

Laurie Segall
CNN Money の技術革新や企業家精神などを扱う科学技術専門の特派員として活躍中。シリコンバレーや、新しいテクノロジーを扱う企業、およびベンチャー・ビジネスなどのニュースを専門としている。ミシガン大学より政治学の学士を取得。

1-04

Laurie Segall: He didn't see me (a) <u>type it</u>, so how did this security (1) <u>researcher</u> (b) <u>figure out</u> my iPad PIN number? Let's take a step (2) <u>back</u>. You're (c) <u>at a</u> coffee shop, reading the iPad. You (1) <u>enter</u> your (2) <u>password</u> and start browsing—pretty basic protocol these days.

【アメリカ英語の発音の特徴】

(1) researcher, enter ▶ /ər/ という発音。[特徴3]
(2) back, password ▶ /æ/ という発音。[特徴1]

【音声変化のポイント】

(a) type it ▶ type の語尾の /p/ と it の語頭の /i/ がつながり「タイピット」と聞こえる。
(b) figure out ▶ figure の語尾の /r/ が、後の out の /a/ とつながり「フィギャラウト」と聞こえる。
(c) at a ▶ at の語尾の /t/ と a の /ə/ がつながり「アタ」と聞こえる。さらに弾音化すると「アラ」のように聞こえる。

Jeanne Moos
ニューヨークを拠点に活躍する全国ニュースの特派員。CNN での 27 年間に、国内および国際的な問題や画期的なニュースなどを担当してきている。

Jeanne Moos: See (1)<u>Derby</u> run. But (a)<u>if you're</u> wondering what's making the clickety-clack—it's his (2)<u>3-D-printer</u> prosthetic legs.

【アメリカ英語の発音の特徴】

(1) Derby ▶ /ər/ という発音。[特徴 3]
(2) 3-D-printer ▶ /ər/ という発音。[特徴 3]

【音声変化のポイント】

(a) if you're ▶ you're の you が /jə/ と弱音で発音され、are も /ər/ と弱音で発音され、これがつながり「イフヤー」と聞こえる。

Natalie Allen
CNN インターナショナルのアンカー兼特派員。1992 年から 2001 年まで CNN でアンカーを務める。また、NBC のアンカーも務めていた。The University of Memphis では政治学の修士号を取得。学生の頃からニュース放送に 25 年携わっている。最近ではニュースの他に 2014 Women's Leadership Conference のホストを務めた。

Natalie Allen: OK, a dog born with (a)<u>deformed legs</u> is getting a second (1)<u>chance</u> at life. As CNN's Jeanne Moos reports, Derby finally can run like other dogs (2)<u>after</u> he was fitted with a custom set of 3-D-printed prosthetics. (b)<u>Take a</u> look.

【アメリカ英語の発音の特徴】

(1) chance ▶ /æ/ という発音。[特徴 1]
(2) after ▶ /ər/ という発音。[特徴 3]

【音声変化のポイント】

(a) deformed legs ▶ deformed の語尾の /d/ が消えて「ディフォームレッグズ」に聞こえる。
(b) take a ▶ take の /k/ と後ろの a の /ə/ がつながり「テイカ」に聞こえる。

Atika Shubert
ロンドンを拠点にしている CNN の特派員。ヨーロッパ、中東、アジアなどの広範囲なレポートを担当している。ボストンのタフツ大学で経済学士号を取得。インドネシア語も話す。

1-07

Atika Shubert: Welcome back to CNN News (1) Center, live from London. If you think (1) turning your smart phone or (2) tablet away from others when you enter your (2) pass code means (a) your PINs safe, well, (b) think again. Laurie Segall shows us how thieves await using a wearable tech to look over your shoulder.

【アメリカ英語の発音の特徴】

(1) Center, turning ▶ /ər/ という発音。［特徴 3］
(2) tablet, pass ▶ /æ/ という発音。［特徴 1］

【音声変化のポイント】

(a) your PINs ▶ your が弱音 /jə/ で発音され /r/ が消えて「ヤピンズ」と聞こえる。
(b) think again ▶ think の /k/ が、後の again の /ə/ とつながり「スィンカゲン」と聞こえる。

Jim Boulden
イギリスで作成される CNN の国際的に配信される番組の記者。アメリカの Maryland 州、Baltimore 生まれ。Pennsylvania の Kutztown University 卒。電子機器による遠距離通信を専攻。副専攻としては政治学を学ぶ。

1-08

Jim Boulden: There's the queen, the red double-decker buses and the red telephone (1) boxes. The (2) first two symbols of Britain (3) are still (a) going strong, but who makes a phone call (b) in a public (1) box anymore? So, (c) what to do with those empty red (1) boxes?

【アメリカ英語の発音の特徴】

(1) boxes ▶ /ɑ/ という発音。［特徴 4］
(2) first ▶ /ər/ という発音。［特徴 3］
(3) are ▶ /ər/ という発音。［特徴 3］

【音声変化のポイント】

(a) going strong ▶ going の語尾の /ɪŋ/ が /ɪn/ となり、「ゴーインスッロング」と聞こえる。
(b) in a ▶ in の /n/ と、後の a がつながり「イナ」と聞こえる。
(c) what to do ▶ what の語尾の /t/ と to の語頭の /t/ がつながり「ワットゥドゥ」と聞こえる。

Samuel Burke
CNN International の a business correspondent。CNN の New York 支局を中心にソーシャル・メディア、ネットワークやアプリなどについての最新ニュースをレポートしている。メキシコの La Universidad Autónoma de Guadalajara でスペイン語の言語学を学び、アリゾナ州立大学を首席で卒業。ウォルター・クロンカイトジャーナリズム学校からジャーナリズムの修士号を取得。

1-09

Samuel Burke: The construction (1)worker, the city businessman, a pilot—(2)all professionals, (2)all male Legos. In the (3)past, if you wanted a professional lady Lego, well, you had to (a)build it yourself. Now, Lego's released a new set called Research Institute, featuring a scientist, (b)an astronomer, even a paleontologist, and all female.

【アメリカ英語の発音の特徴】

(1) worker ▶ /ər/ という発音。[特徴 3]
(2) all ▶ /ɑː/ という発音。[特徴 4]
(3) past ▶ /æ/ という発音。[特徴 1]

【音声変化のポイント】

(a) build it ▶ build の /d/ と it がつながり「ビルディット」と聞こえる。
(b) an astronomer ▶ an の /n/ と astronomer の /ə/ がつながり「アナストロノマー」と聞こえる。

1.3. イギリス英語の発音の主な特徴

[特徴 1] /æ/ という発音

　イギリス英語の最大の特徴としては、/æ/ という発音がアメリカと比べて弱かったり、/ɑː/ という音になったりする。can't は「カーント」と聞こえる。

[特徴2] 綴り字のrを発音しない

　もう一つの大きな特徴は、イギリス英語では、綴り字のrは基本的には発音しないことである。

[特徴3] /əʊ/ という発音

　さらに、アメリカ英語では /oʊ/ と発音される二重母音が、イギリスでは /əʊ/ のように発音されるので、know は「ナウ」のように聞こえる。

[特徴4] /ɔː/ という発音

　また、/ʊə/ (poor)、/oə/ (pour) の発音が、イギリス英語ではいずれも /ɔː/ の音で発音される傾向がある。なので「ポー」と聞こえる。

[特徴5] /t/ や /d/ という音の弾音化がない

　/t/ や /d/ という音が、アメリカ英語のように弾音化されず、はっきり発音される。better は「ベッター」、powder は「パウダー」に、louder は「ラウダー」と聞こえる。

1.4. イギリス英語を使う主なアンカーとレポーター

Nina dos Santos
The Business View with Nina dos Santos のホスト。Imperial College London で理学士号と経済学修士号を取得。英語、フランス語、イタリア語のネイティブ・スピーカーで、ドイツ語とポルトガル語も話す。

1-10

Nina dos Santos: The other thing people who work with me, (1) <u>know</u> me (2) <u>socially</u>, will (1) <u>know</u> is that I'm never (3) <u>far</u> from my little tablet (4) <u>computer</u>, and sometimes—it's (a) <u>got a</u> nice little keyboard that comes out—I start (b) <u>tapping away</u>.

【イギリス英語の発音の特徴】

(1) know ▶ /əʊ/ の発音。[特徴3]
(2) socially ▶ /əʊ/ の発音。[特徴3]
(3) far ▶ 綴り字のrを発音しない。[特徴2]
(4) computer ▶ /t/ という音の弾音化がない。[特徴6]

【音声変化のポイント】

(a) got a ▶ got の /t/ と a がつながって「ゴタ」に聞こえる。
(b) tapping away ▶ tapping の /ɪŋ/ が /ɪn/ となり、away とつながり「タッピンアウェイ」と聞こえる。

Max Foster
CNN International のアンカー兼記者。Cardiff University で経営管理学を学ぶ。Portsmouth の Highbury College より放送ジャーナリズムの postgraduate diploma を取得。

1-11

Max Foster (CNN): Clicking "Like" on Facebook is something (1) (a) <u>most of us</u> do without thinking. Now, a study from the University of Cambridge (b) <u>says the</u> pages you "like" are as revealing as taking a personality test. In (2) <u>fact</u>, some parts of your identity could be predicted with 95 percent (3) <u>accuracy</u>.

【イギリス英語の発音の特徴】

(1) most ▶ /əʊ/ の発音。「マウスト」のように聞こえる。［特徴 3］
(2) fact ▶ 弱い /æ/ の発音。［特徴 1］
(3) accuracy ▶ 弱い /æ/ の発音。［特徴 1］

【音声変化のポイント】

(a) most of us ▶ most と of が、また、of と us が全部つながって発音され「マウスタバス」と聞こえる。
(b) says the ▶ says の /z/ と the の /ð/ が同化されて、「セッザ」と聞こえる。

Matthew Chance
ロンドンを拠点に活躍している CNN の上級海外特派員 (senior international correspondent)。中東、アフガニスタン、ロシアとチュニジア、ヨーロッパと極東についてのニュースのレポートをしている。University of London の東洋アフリカ研究所 (School of Oriental and African Studies) で考古学と芸術 (archaeology and art) の学士を取得。

1-12

Matthew Chance: This is (a) <u>about as</u> Chinese as the Russian (1) <u>capital</u> gets. For generations, the old Perlov Tea House in central Moscow has been supplying its fine blends from the (2) <u>Far</u> East. And today, Russia's thirst (b) <u>for China</u> has never been (3) <u>greater</u>.

【イギリス英語の発音の特徴】

(1) capital ▶ 弱い /æ/ の発音。［特徴1］
(2) Far ▶ 綴り字のrを発音しない。［特徴2］
(3) greater ▶ 綴り字のrを発音しない。［特徴2］

【音声変化のポイント】

(a) about as ▶ about の /t/ と、as がつながって「アバウタズ」と聞こえる。
(b) for China ▶ for の /ɔː/ が弱音化して /ə/ となり「ファチャイナ」と聞こえる。

Isha Sesay
CNN International では CNN NewsCenter のアンカーを担当。シェラレオネ系イギリス人。Cambridge University の Trinity College で英語の学位を取得。優等生として卒業。

1-13

Isha Sesay (CNN): But back in Hubei Province, students at Xiaogang No. 1 High School are (1) hard at work, studying (a) night and day for the notorious exam. (2) More than half the (3) class is taking advantage of the amino-acids IV drip. A bottle of the substance (b) costs about 100 yuan.

【イギリス英語の発音の特徴】

(1) hard ▶ 綴り字のrを発音しない。［特徴2］
(2) More ▶ /ɔː/ という発音。［特徴4］
(3) class ▶ /ɑː/ という発音。［特徴1］

【音声変化のポイント】

(a) night and day ▶ night の /t/ と and がつながり、さらに and の /d/ と day の /d/ が融合して「ナイ(タ)ンディ」と聞こえる。
(b) costs about ▶ costs の /z/ と about がつながり「コスツァバウト」と聞こえる。

Zain Asher
ロンドン生まれのロンドン育ちのナイジェリア人。オックスフォード大学でフランス語とスペイン語を専攻。2006年にコロンビア大学の大学院でジャーナリズムの修士号を取得。メキシコ、フランス、ナイジェリアに住んで働いたことがあり、フランス語、スペイン語、ナイジェリアの方言であるイーボ(Ibo) が流暢に話せる。CNN Newsroom のアンカーを John Vause と一緒に担当している。

Zain Asher: Two hundred thousand people (1) <u>actually</u> (a) <u>applied</u> (2) <u>for this</u>. But the (3) <u>catch</u> is you (b) <u>have to say</u> goodbye to everyone you love.

【イギリス英語の発音の特徴】

Zain Asher の話す英語は、基本的にはイギリス英語である。しかし、「/æ/ という発音がアメリカと比べて弱い」というイギリス英語の特徴がなく、(1) actually や (3) catch の発音では強く発音されている。しかし、(2) for の /r/ は発音されていないので、イギリス英語の特徴を反映している。

【音声変化のポイント】

(a) applied for this ▶ applied の語尾の /d/ が消失して、for が /fə/ と弱音で発音され、「アプライファジス」に聞こえる。
(b) have to say ▶ have が /həf/ と弱音で発音され、to の /uː/ が弱音化して /ə/ となり、「ハフタセィ」と聞こえる。

Clare Sebastian
ケンブリッジ大学でロシア語とドイツ語学士号を取得。現在、CNNのシニア・プロデューサーとして活躍中。

Clare Sebastian: This is the Amos-6, Facebook's latest salvo in the race to bring the Internet to the (1) <u>entire</u> world. Facebook has (a) <u>partnered with</u> French telecoms company Eutelsat (b) <u>to</u> (2) <u>share</u> all the broadband of the Amos-6 satellite.

【イギリス英語の発音の特徴】

(1) entire ▶ 語尾の綴り字の r を発音しない。［特徴2］
(2) share ▶ 語尾の綴り字の r を発音しない。［特徴2］

【音声変化のポイント】

(a) parted with ▶ parted の /ed/ と with の /w/ がつながって「パーテッドゥイズ」に聞こえる。
(b) to share ▶ to の /ə/ が弱まり、share とつながり「トゥシャー」と聞こえる。

1.5. オーストラリア英語の発音の主な特徴

　方言は地方によって分類されるより、階級や学歴で分類されることが多い。イギリスの容認発音 (RP) に近い Cultivated、これは 10% の人々が話すと言われている。オーストラリアの大半の人が話す General、これが一般的にオーストラリア英語として紹介されている。また、30% の人が話すと言われている Broad とよばれる発音があり、/aɪ/ が General より顕著に /ɔi/ に近く発音される。

[特徴 1] /æɪ/ という発音

　today が to die のように聞こえるのが有名だ。アメリカ英語の /ei/ がオーストラリア英語では /æɪ/ (「エイ」が「アイ」) と発音される。

[特徴 2] /ɑi/, /ɑe/ という発音

　アメリカ英語の /aɪ/ が /ɑi/, /ɑe/ (「アイ」が「オイ」) と発音される。buy が boy のように聞こえる。

[特徴 3] /æɔ/ という発音

　/aʊ/ が /æɔ/ のように発音される。loud は「ロウド」のように聞こえる。

[特徴 4] 語尾の r は発音しない

　イギリス英語と同じく、語尾の r は発音しない。

1.6. オーストラリア英語を使う主なアンカーとレポーター

Andrew Stevens
CNN International のアンカー兼特派員。毎日の *World Business Today* の共同司会者をしている。CNN に入社するまで CNBC Asia の上級特派員 (senior correspondent) や香港の新聞 *The South China Morning Post* の金融記事の編集者を歴任。オーストラリア生まれ。

1-16

Andrew Stevens: Working mothers in Japan still (1) <u>face</u> enormous challenges in 2014, (a) <u>and as</u> our Will Ripley reports, some women (2) <u>say</u> (3) <u>they</u> feel (b) <u>forced to</u> sacrifice their careers if they want to have children.

【オーストラリア英語の発音の特徴】

(1) face ▶ /ei/ が /æɪ/ と発音される。「ファイス」に聞こえる。[特徴 1]

(2) say ▶ /ei/ が /æɪ/ と発音される。「サイ」に聞こえる。[特徴1]
(3) they ▶ /ei/ が /æɪ/ と発音される。「ザイ」に聞こえる。[特徴1]

【音声変化のポイント】

(a) and as ▶ and の語尾の /d/ と as の /ə/ がつながって「アンダズ」と聞こえる。
(b) forced to ▶ forced の語尾の /t/ が消えて「フォーストゥ」と聞こえる。

John Vause
オーストラリア出身のジャーナリスト。CNN International の Atlanta 駐在員。CNN に入る前にはオーストラリアの the Seven Network in Australia の Los Angeles 支局の支局長だった。

1-17

John Vause: So, now, they're looking (1) for candidates to (2) go and live on Mars. And the good thing (a) about this is that it's a one-way trip—you never come back. And there's a lot of people who I think (b) should apply.

【オーストラリア英語の発音の特徴】

(1) for ▶ 語尾の r は発音しない。[特徴4]
(2) go ▶ /æɔ/ という発音。[特徴3]

【音声変化のポイント】

(a) about this ▶ about の /t/ が消えて「アバウディス」と聞こえる。
(b) should apply ▶ should の語尾の /d/ と apply の /ə/ がつながって「シュダプライ」と聞こえる。

Michael Holmes
CNN インターナショナルのアンカー兼特派員。*International Desk* のアンカーを担当している。Yale University で歴史学の学士、Medill School of Journalism より Master of Science in Journalism を取得。

1-18

Michael Holmes: These 100 applicants will now (1) go on (2) for further testing, including team-building exercises and isolation testing. The journey to Mars will (3) take about seven months. But (a) for those chosen, it's the biggest decision (b) of their life.

xviii

【オーストラリア英語の発音の特徴】

(1) go ▶ /aʊ/ が /æɔ/ のように発音される。「ガゥ」に聞こえる。[特徴1]
(2) for ▶ 綴り字の r は発音しない。[特徴4]
(3) take ▶ /ei/ が /æɪ/ と発音される。「タイク」に聞こえる。[特徴1]

【音声変化のポイント】

(a) for those ▶ for の /ɔː/ が弱音化され /ə/ となり、「ファゾーズ」と聞こえる。
(b) of their life ▶ their が弱音化され /ðə/ となり「オヴザライフ」と聞こえる。

Rosemary Church
北アイルランドの Belfast 生まれ。8歳までロンドンで過ごし、その後、家族と一緒にオーストラリアに移住。Australian National University 卒。文学士。University of Canberra の大学院でメディアと法律で修士号を取得。

1-19

Rosemary Church: Nearly a (1) <u>decade</u> after Indonesia's killer tsunami swept a 4-year-old girl (a) <u>and her</u> 7-year-old brother (b) <u>out to sea</u> and almost certain death, the girl is back with her parents. Our Ralitsa Vassileva brings us an (2) <u>amazing</u> story of faith, survival and love.

【オーストラリア英語の発音の特徴】

Rosemary Church の話す英語は、オーストラリアの中でも cultivated に属す英語で、イギリス英語に非常に近い英語である。そのため、先に上げたオーストラリア英語の general の特徴が現れていない。例えば (1) decade は、general では /dekæɪd/ と発音されるが、彼女の発音を聞くと /dekeɪd/ となっている。同じように (2) amazing の発音も /æɪ/ でなく /ei/ となっていて、一般に言われるオーストラリア英語の特徴はこの人の発音からは察知できない。

【音声変化のポイント】

(a) and her ▶ and が弱音で /ənd/ と発音され、her も弱音で /ər/ と発音されているので「アンダー」と聞こえる。
(b) out to see ▶ out の /t/ が消えて、後ろの to の /tuː/ が /tə/ と弱音化され、「アウタスィー」と聞こえる。

1.7. カナダ英語の発音の主な特徴

　発音の面から見るとカナダ英語、特にカナダ西部の発音はアメリカ英語とほとんど同じだと言ってよい。アメリカ英語と同じように /æ/ という発音をしているし /r/ を響かせて発音する。カナダ東部ではイギリス英語に近い発音も残っている。他の英語で見られない特徴としては、Tronto という地名をアメリカ英語では /tərontou/ と発音するが、カナダ英語では /tərono/ という風に /t/ が /n/ にかわる。

1.8. カナダ英語を使う主なアンカー

Paula Newton
カナダを本拠地とする CNN の国際特派員。2005 年に CNN に入社する以前は 12 年間カナダの CTV のアナウンサーをしていた。オンタリオの McMaster University で経営管理学（国際金融）で修士号を取得。オタワの Carleton University よりジャーナリズム・政治学名誉学士号を取得。英語、フランス語、イタリア語を駆使し、ロシア語やスペイン語も話せる。

1-20

Paula Newton: Now, (1) <u>for</u> many people, Lego was (a) <u>one of the</u> building blocks of childhood. And now, the Danish company that makes it is breaking away from those gender stereotypes, (2) <u>apparently</u>—get this—after it was (b) <u>told off</u> by a 7-year-old. Samuel Burke has the details.

【カナダ英語の発音の特徴】

(1) for ▶ /r/ を響かせる発音。
(2) apparently ▶ /æ/ という発音。

【音声変化のポイント】

(a) one of the ▶ one の /n/ と of の /əv/ がつながり「ワナブザ」と聞こえる。
(b) told off ▶ told の語尾の /d/ と off の /ɔ/ がつながり、「トールドフ」と聞こえる。

Unit 1

Well Suited for Royalty

　2017年11月、イギリス王室の次男坊ハリー王子の婚約が発表された。お相手はアメリカ人俳優メーガン・マークルさん。交際中、彼女の出自や離婚歴がゴシップ紙をにぎわせたが、王子は毅然として抗議。めでたくエリザベス女王の許可も得た。2人のなれ初めやメーガンさんの人物像のほか、ダイアナ妃の死を王子がどのように乗り越えたかについても、彼自身の言葉でお伝えする。

 **Warm Up**

【聴き取りのポイント】

下線部に注意しながら、聴いてみよう。

 Meghan Markle will be the first American to marry into the royal family since Wallis Simpson famously wed King Edward VIII 81 years ago.

ポイント

下線部の読み方に注目しよう。

【内容理解のポイント】

次の文を考えてみよう。

It was a long-distance affair at first(1), with Markle based in Toronto(2), where *Suits* is filmed.

ポイント

1. 下線部 (1) の "at first" と "first" の違いは何かを考えてみよう。
2. 下線部 (2) を節（接続詞＋主語＋述語）の形に直してみよう。

Words and Phrases to Study

back off	bring up
engagement	imminent
monarchy	philanthropy
relevant	tabloid
undertone	unprecedented

Definition

engagement 1. an agreement between two people to marry

_____ 2. the practice of giving money and help to people who are poor or in trouble

_____ 3. a newspaper that has small pages, a lot of photographs, and stories mainly about sex, famous people, etc., rather than serious news

_____ 4. a feeling or quality that is not directly expressed but can still be recognized

_____ 5. never having happened before, or never having happened so much

_____ 6. to move backwards, away from someone or something; to stay away from

_____ 7. likely to happen very soon

_____ 8. to mention a subject or start to talk about it

_____ 9. the system in which a country is ruled by a king or queen

_____ 10. directly relating to the subject or problem being discussed or considered

Examples

1. Tourists visiting Kensington Palace were overjoyed to find that they had chosen the very day on which the _engagement_ was announced.

2. This is a species the population of which has become so severely reduced that the animal is in _____ danger of becoming extinct.

3. Before you mention that very delicate matter, consider not only what your intention is in _____ the topic but also what sort of response you can expect.

4. Many business leaders altogether ignore the topic of _____, on the grounds their most urgent concern is no longer social responsibility but, instead, competitiveness.

5. To cover the costs of political campaigning, which have by now risen to a height that would have been quite unimaginable only thirty years ago, the president is presently spending a[n] _____ amount of time on fundraising.

6. When nothing really important is happening, _____ journalists will dig up old scandals for the sake of being able to use sensational headlines.

7. Some British people believe the country no longer needs a _____.

8. When Shanti let her tame mongoose loose, the python that had appeared in her garden _____ in a hurry.

9. Donald J. Trump frequently comes under fire for the racist _____ to his speeches.

10. A total of nine articles from the two databases proved _____ to the current question of gendered Internet use.

「英王室のやんちゃ王子」として知られ、これまで数々の浮き名を流してきたハリー王子ことヘンリー・オブ・ウェールズ 王子が、2017年11月27日、アメリカ人女優メーガン・マークルさんとの婚約を発表した。デイリーメール紙やニューズウィーク誌などのマスコミでは、メーガンさんがアフリカ系の血を引いたバイレイシャル (bi-racial) であることや離婚歴があることが取り沙汰されたが、レポートにもあるように、王子は声明文で強く抗議。王室自体も歓迎ムードだ。結婚式は、2018年5月19日にウィンザー城の聖ジョージ礼拝堂 (St George's Chapel at Windsor Castle) で執り行われた。

Blanks to Fill in

Fill in the blanks with suitable words.

Kristie Lu Stout (Anchor):

Breaking news of a royal engagement: Prince Harry is set to marry American actress Meghan Markle in the spring. Max Foster has more.

Max Foster (Reporter):

They may be an unconventional couple when it comes to the monarchy, but by all accounts, this marriage is welcomed by the royal family.

Meghan Markle will be (1)_____ (2)_____ (3)_____ (4)_____ marry into the royal family since Wallis Simpson famously wed King Edward VIII 81 years ago, forcing his abdication from the throne. As was Simpson, Markle is divorced. Born and raised in Los Angeles by her African-American mother and white father, she rose to fame (5)_____ (6)_____ (7)_____ (8)_____ (9)_____ of the American TV show, *Suits*.

It was a long-distance affair at first, with Markle based in Toronto, where *Suits* is filmed. The relationship was kept mostly under wraps until tabloid attacks on her background, prompted Prince Harry to take the unprecedented step (10)_____ (11)_____ (12)_____ (13)_____ (14)_____, warning the press to back off his girlfriend. Calling out one tabloid for racial undertones, Harry said a line had been crossed.

(15)_____ (16)_____ (17)_____ (18)_____ *Vanity Fair* magazine, Markle said the couple met in London in July 2016. They were introduced by a mutual friend, reportedly at Harry's request, and quickly learned they share philanthropy (19)_____ (20)_____ (21)_____ (22)_____.

Meghan Markle (at UN Women Conference, 2015)**:**

Women make up more than half of the world's population and potential, so it is neither just nor practical for their voices—for our voices— (23)_____ (24)_____ (25)_____ at the highest levels of decision making.

Max Foster:

Along with the Duke and Duchess of Cambridge, Harry has worked to raise awareness of mental health, recently speaking about the effects (26)_____ (27)_____ (28)_____ (29)_____ (30)_____ Diana had on him.

Prince Henry [Harry] (Duke OF Sussex, speaking with the Duke and Duchess of Cambridge in *Heads Together* video):

1-26
1-31

I always thought to myself, you know, "What's the point in bringing up the past? What's the point in bringing up something that's only going to make you sad? It ain't going to change it. It ain't going to bring her back." And when you start thinking like that, it can really be damaging.

Max Foster:

Talk of an engagement ramped up when Markle quit her job on *Suits* in October. When she was pictured with her dogs in London, a move to Kensington Palace looked imminent. In a time when the monarchy is eager to stay relevant, Meghan Markle could ⁽³¹⁾_____ ⁽³²⁾_____ ⁽³³⁾_____ ⁽³⁴⁾_____ ⁽³⁵⁾_____ ⁽³⁶⁾_____.

Max Foster, CNN, London.

✏️ Notes

(Title) (be) **suited for**「〜にふさわしい」(メーガンさんが出演していたドラマの題 "Suits" にかけている) (Title) **royalty**「王族」

p. 5
(l. 2) **breaking news**「速報、今入ったばかりのニュース」 (l. 2) **be set to do**「〜することになっている」 (l. 5) **unconventional**「慣例にとらわれない、型破りな」 (l. 5) **when it comes to**「〜に関するかぎり、〜の話となると」 (l. 6) **by all accounts**「誰に聞いても」 (l. 6) **be welcomed**「歓迎される」 (l. 8) **Wallis Simpson**「ウォリス・シンプソン」(現エリザベス女王の伯父エドワーズ8世は、人妻でアメリカ人のシンプソン夫人(後に離婚)と大恋愛のすえ、王位を捨て結婚。「王冠を賭けた恋」として知られる) (l. 9) **wed**「〜と結婚する、結ばれる」 (l. 9) **abdication**「(王位などの) 放棄、退位」 (l. 11) **rise to fame**「有名になる、世に知られるようになる」 (l. 13) *Suits*「SUITS/ スーツ」(人気リーガルドラマ。メーガンさんの役はパラリーガル(弁護士志望の法律事務職員))

p. 6
(l. 1) **long-distance affair**「遠距離恋愛」 (l. 2) **keep ... under wraps**「〜を隠しておく、表沙汰にしない」 (l. 3) **prompt ... to do**「〜を刺激して〜させる」 (l. 4) **take the step of doing**「〜するという処置をとる、手段をとる」 (l. 6) **call out**「〜を非難する、とがめる、〜の誤りを指摘する」 (l. 6) **undertone**「含意、含み」 (l. 7) **cross a line**「一線を超える、度が過ぎる」 (l. 8) *Vanity Fair*『バニティ・フェア』(文化、ファッション、政治などを扱うアメリカの総合月刊誌) (l. 10) **mutual friend**「共通の友人」 (l. 13) **UN Women**(国連の女性関連4組織を統合して2011年に発足した新組織) (l. 14) **make up**「〜(の割合)を占める」 (l. 16) **decision making**「意思決定」 (l. 20) **raise awareness of ...**「〜に対する意識を高める」 (l. 20) **have an effect on ...**「〜に影響を及ぼす」

p. 7
(l. 1) **the Duke and Duchess of Cambridge**「ケンブリッジ公爵夫妻」(ハリー王子の兄であるウィリアム王子とキャサリン妃夫妻のこと) (l. 2) **Heads Together**「ヘッズ・トゥゲザー」(ウィリアム王子とキャサリン妃、そしてハリー王子が設立したメンタルヘルスに関する慈善団体) (l. 3) **think to oneself**「密かに考える、心の内で思う」 (l. 3) **What's the point in doing?**「〜して何になるのか、どんな意味があるのか、〜しても無駄だ」 (l. 5) **change it**(この it は「状況」のこと) (l. 6) **damaging**「有害な、ダメージを与える」 (l. 8) **ramp up**「増す、高まる」 (l. 9) **picture**「(新聞・雑誌などに) 〜の写真を掲載する」 (l. 10) **Kensington Palace**「ケンジントン宮殿」(ケンブリッジ公爵夫妻をはじめとする英王室のメンバーが居住する宮殿) (l. 10) **be eager to do**「しきりに〜したがる、〜することに意欲的である」

Judgments to Make

[T / F] 1. Though the engagement of Prince Harry and Megan Markle may not conventional, it is said to be welcomed by the Royal Family.

[T / F] 2. Megan Markle will be the first-ever American to marry into the Royal Family.

[T / F] 3. Megan's parents are both African-Americans.

[T / F] 4. When a tabloid attacked Megan in relation to her background, Prince Harry warned the press to back off.

[T / F] 5. It is reported that Prince Harry and Megan met through a mutual friend.

[T / F] 6. Megan said at a conference that women should be involved in decision-making processes at the highest levels.

[T / F] 7. In his speech, Prince Harry implied that his interest in raising awareness of mental health was connected with the effects of his mother's death on his own mind.

[T / F] 8. The press refrained from talking about a possible engagement even when Megan quit her job on *Suits*.

 Partial Composition

1. 民族「純化」の名目で何万人もの罪のない人々が殺戮されるのを見たとき、私は一線を越えたと思いました。

   I thought that _____ we saw tens of thousands of innocent people being killed in the name of ethnic 'cleansing'.

2. 彼は、環境問題、とりわけその地域の森林破壊に関して、意識を高めたいと願っています。

   He is hoping to _____, particularly regarding deforestation in the region.

Unit 1: Well Suited for Royalty   9

Unit 2

Never More Timely

2017年のノーベル平和賞に、核兵器廃絶国際キャンペーン (ICAN) が選ばれた。ICANは世界100カ国を超える約470の市民団体からなる国際NGOで、同年7月に国連で採択された「核兵器禁止条約」の成立に貢献したことが評価された。北朝鮮情勢が不安定で、核の脅威が高まる中での受賞となったが、この賞は、ノーベル委員会から世界へ向けての明確なメッセージと言えるだろう。

 **Warm Up**

【聴き取りのポイント】

下線部に注意しながら、聴いてみよう。

 The Nobel Committee has honored the notion of a world free of nuclear weapons before, awarding the prize in 2005 to the International Atomic Energy Agency, the IAEA, for its efforts to prevent the spread of nuclear weapons.

> ポイント

下線部に注意して聴いたうえで、自分で発音してみよう。

【内容理解のポイント】

次の文を考えてみよう。

Not since the Cold War has the threat from nuclear weapons seemed so acute.

> ポイント

1. 下線部（述語）に対応する主語はどれだろうか？
2. 文全体を訳してみよう。

Words and Phrases to Study

acute	ally
ban	belligerent
coalition	consequence
humanitarian	civilian
slaughter	treaty

Definition

slaughter 1. a killing of a large number of people in a violent and cruel way

_____ 2. a group newly formed by people from several different groups, who have joined together to achieve a particular purpose, usually a political one

_____ 3. a country that agrees to help or support another country, especially in a war

_____ 4. concerned with improving bad living conditions and preventing unfair treatment of people and animals

_____ 5. a formal written agreement recognized by two or more countries or governments

_____ 6. an official order that prevents something from being used or done

_____ 7. something that happens as a result of a particular action or set of conditions

_____ 8. very serious

_____ 9. very unfriendly and wanting to argue or fight

_____ 10. anyone who is not a member of military forces or a police-force

Examples

1. This discriminatory policy soon led to a massive _slaughter_ of those that belonged to the tribe hated by the government.

2. Finland, as one of Nazi Germany's _____, concluded a separate peace-agreement with the Soviet Union.

3. Since _____ compose the largest proportion of the population, their right to control use of Self-defense Forces is a matter that, in a democracy, lawmakers have a duty to confirm.

4. After being out for hours in the freezing cold, she developed an _____ case of pneumonia.

5. While the President is _____ on the world-scene, he dislikes confrontations at home.

6. It appears to be somewhat easier to raise private funds for _____ causes, when these are related to natural disasters.

7. President Donald Trump says Republicans are "going to win" in this year's midterm elections—and warns of dire _____ if they don't.

8. WHO has urged governments to protect the world's young people by imposing a _____ on all tobacco-advertising.

9. A _____-government is formed when two or more political parties join forces in order to create a majority.

10. Although no specific deadline for concluding a peace-_____ between Russia and Japan has been established, a determination to reach such a conclusion is shared by the two countries.

スイスのジュネーブ (Geneva) に本部を置く ICAN は 200 年に結成され、核兵器を法的に禁止して廃絶することを目指している。2017 年 10 月時点で 101 カ国 468 団体が参加。国際会議で各国政府に盛んに働きかけを行い、メディアとインターネットを使ったキャンペーンを精力的に展開して、核兵器を非合法化する条約の制定に力を注いできた。その努力が実を結び、2017 年 7 月に核兵器の開発・実験・保有・使用などを全面的に禁止する国際条約 (The Treaty on the Prohibition of Nuclear Weapons (TPNW)) が採択された。

　この核兵器禁止条約には 100 カ国以上が加盟する見通しだが、米英仏などの核保有国側は「国際安全保障の現実を無視しており、解決にならない」と強く反発。アメリカの核抑止力に頼る日本も、条約に署名する意思がないことを明言している。

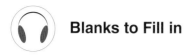 Blanks to Fill in

Fill in the blanks with suitable words.

Natalie Allen (Anchor):

1-33
1-38

The 2017 Nobel Peace Prize winner was announced Friday. It went to an organization which the Nobel Committee says works to "draw attention to the catastrophic humanitarian consequences of any use of nuclear weapons." As CNN's Diana Magnay reports, it is especially timely given today's political climate.

Diana Magnay (Reporter):

1-34
1-39

Not since the Cold War (1)_____ (2)_____ (3)_____ (4)_____ (5)_____ (6)_____ seemed so acute: North Korea's young leader dangerously flippant with his nuclear threats; the U.S. president worryingly belligerent in his response; and now, the talk from Washington that he might scupper the Iran deal, struck in July 2015 in a bid to curb Iran's nuclear weapons program.

Perhaps that's what he meant on Thursday by this:

U.S. President Donald Tramp (at White House photo-opportunity):

The calm before the storm.

Unidentified Reporter:

What storm, Mr. President?

Donald Trump:

You'll find out.

Diana Magnay:

The Iran deal's key architects had been hot favorites to win this year's Nobel Peace Prize. It went instead to the little-known International Campaign to Abolish Nuclear Weapons, or ICAN, a coalition of NGOs in more than 100 countries working towards a ban on nuclear weapons.

Beatrice Fihn (Executive Director, ICAN):

I think it sends a … sends a message to all nuclear-armed states, and all states ⁽⁷⁾_____ ⁽⁸⁾_____ ⁽⁹⁾_____ ⁽¹⁰⁾_____ ⁽¹¹⁾_____ ⁽¹²⁾_____ ⁽¹³⁾_____ for security that it is unacceptable behavior. We will not support it. We will not make excuses for it. You can't threaten to indiscriminately slaughter hundreds of thousands of civilians in the name of security.

Diana Magnay:

This prize [is] a recognition of ICAN's work pushing for a treaty on ⁽¹⁴⁾_____ ⁽¹⁵⁾_____ ⁽¹⁶⁾_____ ⁽¹⁷⁾_____ ⁽¹⁸⁾_____, adopted by 122 nations at the UN in July, the world's nine nuclear states, including the U.S., and some of their key allies, refusing to sign.

The prize today, said the executive director of ICAN, [is] a tribute to (19)_____ (20)_____ (21)_____ Nagasaki and Hiroshima and to (22)_____ (23)_____ (24)_____ nuclear testing all around the world, and a rebuke to the nuclear powers.

Beatrice Fihn:

The first step to addressing North Korea is to also stop behaving in the same way.

Diana Magnay:

The Nobel Committee has honored the notion of (25)_____ (26)_____ (27)_____ (28)_____ (29)_____ (30)_____ be- fore, awarding the prize in 2005 to the International Atomic Energy Agency, the IAEA, for its efforts to prevent the spread of nuclear weapons— this year's winner (31)_____ (32)_____ (33)_____ (34)_____ (35)_____ (36)_____ that they believe an outright ban, not the nuclear deterrent, will better safeguard peace.

Diana Magnay, CNN, London.

✏️ Notes

p. 14
(l. 2) **Nobel Peace Prize**「ノーベル平和賞」　(l. 2) **winner**「受賞者」　(l. 2) **announce**「発表する」　(l. 2) **go to ...**「(賞などが) ~に与えられる、贈られる」　(l. 3) **Nobel Committee**「ノーベル委員会」　(l. 3) **draw attention to ...**「~に注意を引く」　(l. 4) **catastrophic**「壊滅的な、悲惨な」　(l. 4) **nuclear weapon**「核兵器」　(l. 5) **given**「~を考えると、考慮すれば」　(l. 6) **political climate**「政治情勢」　(l. 8) **the Cold War**「東西冷戦」　(l. 10) **flippant**「軽率な、不真面目な」　(l. 10) **threat**「1. 脅威になるもの 2. 脅迫、おどし」　(l. 11) **worryingly**「心配なほどに」　(l. 11) **belligerent**「好戦的な」　(l. 11) **talk**「うわさ、話」　(l. 12) **scupper**「(計画などを) 台無しにする、ダメにする」　(l. 12) **Iran deal**「イラン核合意」(イランの核開発をめぐり、2015年に米英仏独ロの6カ国とイランが最終合意した行動計画)　(l. 12) **strike**「(契約などを) 取り決める、締結する」　(l. 12) **in a bid to do**「~しようと努力して」　(l. 13) **curb**「~を抑制する、制限する」

p. 15
(l. 4) **find out**「知る、わかる」　(l. 6) **architect**「立案者」　(l. 6) **hot favorite**「有力候補、本命」　(l. 7) **International Campaign to Abolish Nuclear Weapons**「核兵器廃絶国際キャンペーン」(略称 ICAN)　(l. 8) **NGO** = nongovernmental organization「非政府組織」　(l. 14) **make excuse for ...**「~の言い訳をする、弁解をする」　(l. 15) **threaten to do**「~すると脅かす」　(l. 15) **indiscriminately**「見境なく、無差別に」　(l. 16) **in the name of ...**「~の名の下に、名目で」　(l. 18) **push for ...**「~を強く求める」　(l. 20) **the UN** = United Nations「国際連合、国連」

p. 16
(l. 1) **tribute**「敬意・賞賛の印、捧げ物」　(l. 4) **rebuke**「叱責、強い避難」　(l. 4) **nuclear power**「核保有国」　(l. 6) **address**「~に対処する、取り組む」　(l. 9) **honor**「~を高く評価する」　(l. 9) **notion**「考え、見解」　(l. 11) **award A to B**「A (賞など) をBに授与する」　(l. 11) **the International Atomic Energy Agency**「国際原子力機関」(略称 IAEA)　(l. 12) **prevent**「~を防ぐ、阻む」　(l. 14) **outright**「徹底的な、全くの、完全な」　(l. 14) **nuclear deterrent**「核抑止力」　(l. 15) **safeguard**「~を守る、保護する」

Judgments to Make

[T / F] 1. The 2017 Nobel Peace Prize went to an organization that is working to draw attention to the terrible effects of use of nuclear weapons.

[T / F] 2. The current threat from nuclear weapons is not as serious as it was during the Cold War days.

[T / F] 3. Both North Korea's leader and the U.S. president are adamant that they will continue to use nuclear weapons as a threat.

[T / F] 4. As had been expected, the key figures in the Iran deal won this year's Nobel Peace Prize.

[T / F] 5. ICAN is a coalition of NGOs working together to abolish nuclear weapons.

[T / F] 6. According to Beatrice Fihn, the fact that ICAN has been awarded the Nobel Peace Prize can act as a clear message to nuclear-armed states and the like that nuclear armament is no longer acceptable.

[T / F] 7. A treaty to ban nuclear weapons was adopted by 122 nations that included some key allies of the U.S.

[T / F] 8. The Nobel Committee is obviously conveying the message that a complete ban of nuclear weapons will better realize world peace than can the nuclear deterrent.

 Partial Composition

1. リベラル派は人道主義的名のもとで戦争に出て行くが、保守派は国益のために出ていく。

   Liberals will go to war _____ causes, while conservatives will do so for the sake of national interest.

2. 二国間の絆の強化を目指して、両国の首脳がパリで会談を行った。

   The leaders met and talked in Paris _____ the ties between the two countries.

Unit 3

Miracle Transformer

　映画『ウィンストン・チャーチル/ヒトラーから世界を救った男』で特殊メイクを担当した日本人アーティストの辻一弘氏が、第90回アカデミー賞で、日本人として初めてメイクアップ＆ヘアスタイリング賞に輝いた。辻氏は2012年に映画界を引退し、巨大な胸像を作る芸術家として活動していたが、主演のゲイリー・オールドマンから直々のオファーを受け、同作品に参加し、彼をチャーチルに見事に大変身させた。CNNがその制作過程を追った

 **Warm Up**

【聴き取りのポイント】

下線部に注意しながら、聴いてみよう。

1. The extraordinary transformation from greyhound to bulldog began here in an artist's studio in Los Angeles.
2. Once upon a time, he used to work in the movies.
3. This could be once in a lifetime.

● ポイント

下線部の音のつながりに気をつけながら聴いてみよう。

【内容理解のポイント】

次の文を考えてみよう。

However great his performance(1), he didn't become Prime Minister on his own(2).

● ポイント

1. 下線部 (1) の意味を考えよう。
2. 下線部 (2) の意味を考えよう。

Words and Phrases to Study

coax	consecutive
contingent on	extraordinary
figure	meticulous
not exactly	prosthetic
sculptor	special-effect

Definition

coax   1. to persuade someone to do something that they do not want to do by talking to them in a kind, gentle, and patient way

_____   2. an artificial body-part

_____   3. dependent on something that may or may not happen in the future

_____   4. an unusual image or sound that has been produced artificially, in order to be used in a movie or television program

_____   5. someone who shapes stone, wood, clay, metal, etc., in order to make a work of art that is a three-dimensional figure or object

_____   6. following one after the other without any interruptions

_____   7. very careful about even small details

_____   8. very unusual or surprising

_____   9. someone who is important or famous in some way

_____   10. very far from actually being

Examples

1. Sam being very shy, we had to _coax_ him into singing with the girls.
2. Nicole Kidman has rather a snub nose; so, when in the movie *The Hours* she played the real-life writer Virginia Woolf, whose nose was perfectly straight, she used a _____.
3. He's just turned fifty, so he's _____ a young man any more.
4. It is the annual rainy season here, and it has now been raining for five _____ days.
5. Eiji Tsuburaya is known as the man put in charge of _____ for *Godzilla*.
6. It was the _____ Michelangelo that produced the world's most famous image of a totally-naked young man; his *David*.
7. Chris was always punctual, so his being late that morning was quite _____.
8. Everyone was surprised when one of the country's key political _____ announced that he would retire from public life.
9. She is so _____ about everything that, when she made that mistake, I immediately knew something must be wrong with her.
10. Further investment must be made _____ the company's profit-performance.

　京都出身の辻一弘さんが、2018年、第90回アカデミー賞でメイクアップ＆ヘアスタイル賞を受賞した。日本人の個人での受賞は、『ドラキュラ』(Bram Stoker's Dracula)（ゲイリー・オールドマン主演）で1993年に衣裳デザイン賞(Best Costume Design)を受賞した石岡瑛子さんに続いて二人目である。京都出身の辻さんは、1969年生まれで、LA在住48歳。『スター・ウォーズ』(Star Wars)で特撮にはまり、特殊メイク・アーティストとして日本で活動したのち、27歳で渡米。特殊メイクの巨匠ディック・スミスに師事し、その後、兄弟子のリック・ベイカーの工房で『メン・イン・ブラック』(Men in Black)、『もしも昨日が選べたら』(Click)、『マッド・ファット・ワイフ』(Norbit)などの特殊効果やメイクを手がけ、これまでにも2度、アカデミー賞にノミネートされている。

Blanks to Fill in

Fill in the blanks with suitable words.

Rosemary Church (Anchor):

His performance as Sir Winston Churchill in the film *Darkest Hour* has already won 26 awards, including the Golden Globe, Screen Actors Guild and BAFTA trophies for best actor. One might assume that Gary Oldman is the favorite to find himself back on stage at the awards-season grand final—the Oscars, of course, we're talking about—but however great his performance, he didn't become prime minister on his own. CNN's Nick Glass spoke to the makeup artist who came out of retirement to transform the actor into Churchill.

Nick Glass (Reporter):

So, how did they do it? How was Winston Churchill reincarnated so convincingly by Gary Oldman? On the face of it, even in the shadows, the actor and politician don't ⁽¹⁾_____ ⁽²⁾_____ ⁽³⁾_____.

Kazuhiro Tsuji (Makeup Artist):

Gary is...looks like a greyhound, but Churchill ⁽⁴⁾_____ ⁽⁵⁾_____ ⁽⁶⁾_____ ⁽⁷⁾_____.

Nick Glass:

The extraordinary transformation from greyhound to bulldog began here in an artist's studio in Los Angeles. Kazuhiro Tsuji is a sculptor of hyperrealist faces. He likes to recreate historical figures—(8)_____ (9)_____ (10)_____ (11)_____. But once upon a time, he used to work in the movies.

Gary Oldman (Actor, at a panel discussion)**:**

I needed not only a makeup artist, but I needed an *artist*, I felt, for this. And I remember saying, 'There's only one man, Kazuhiro Tsuji.' My playing Winston was really contingent on Kazu.

Nick Glass:

Kazu, as he's known, created the makeup for Jim Carrey in *How the Grinch Stole Christmas* and for Brad Pitt in *The Curious Case of Benjamin Button*, but in 2012, he decided (12)_____ (13)_____ (14)_____ (15)_____.

Kazuhiro Tsuji:

I love to do special-effects makeup, but it was stressing me too much, to the level that I felt like I'm shorten…shortening my life.

Nick Glass:

So Gary Oldman had to coax Kazu back just (16)_____ (17)_____ (18)_____ (19)_____.

Kazuhiro Tsuji:

I never had a[n] opportunity to do a historical character in a film, like, a main character with makeup, and I felt like, 'OK, well, this could be once in a lifetime.'

Nick Glass:

Under the liquid resin, Gary Oldman (20)_____ (21)_____ (22)_____ (23)_____. This process gave Kazu the mold for a life cast, and from that, he began to design the prosthetics.

Kazuhiro Tsuji:

This is the neck. It's like a hood piece that goes over his head.

Nick Glass:

Kazu did the tests on Oldman himself, everything like real skin, including a prosthetic Adam's apple. In all, he designed six pieces, including (24)_____, (25)_____ (26)_____ (27)_____. Kazu left the meticulous daily application to British colleagues David Malinowski and Lucy Sibbick. The process took them (28)_____ (29)_____ (30)_____ (31)_____ every day for 48 consecutive shooting days. Kazu made a series of wigs from baby hair and Angora-rabbit fur.

Kazuhiro Tsuji:

(32)_____ (33)_____ (34)_____ (35)_____ Gary is, like, he just disappears. After 10 minutes, I start to forget about the makeup and start to forget about Gary, because it just…just became Churchill. And that's (36)_____ (37)_____.

Nick Glass:

Nick Glass for CNN, with Kazu Tsuji.

✎ Notes

p. 23

(l. 2) **Winston Churchill**「ウィンストン・チャーチル（1874年–1965年）」（第二次世界大戦中の英国を勝利に導いたことで知られる英国の政治家・首相。BBCが2002年に行った「偉大な英国人」投票で1位に選ばれるなど英国では国民的な人気を誇っている人物。また、ノンフィクション作家としての活動でも知られ、1953年にはノーベル文学賞を受賞）

(l. 2) *Darkest Hour*『ウィンストン・チャーチル／ヒトラーから世界を救った男』（2017年のジョー・ライト監督作品。アカデミー主演男優賞、メイクアップ＆ヘアスタイリング賞など、さまざまな賞に輝いた）　(l. 3) **Golden Globe (Awards)**「ゴールデングローブ賞」（ハリウッド外国人記者協会が選定する映画とテレビの賞）　(l. 3) **Screen Actors Guild**「全米映画俳優組合」（全米映画俳優組合賞を運営している）　(l. 4) **BAFTA**「英国映画テレビ芸術アカデミー、バフタ」（英国アカデミー賞（BAFTA賞とも呼ばれる）を授与している）

(l. 4) **One might assume that …**「〜だと思っても差し支えないだろう」　(l. 5) **favorite**「大本命」　(l. 5) **awards-season**「アウォードシーズンの」（ここでは毎年、年末から翌年3月までの、各種の映画賞が発表される時期を指す。真打ちがアカデミー賞）　(l. 6) **the Oscars**「アカデミー賞授賞式」　(l. 7) **on one's own**「独力で、単独で」　(l. 8) **come out of retirement**「引退から現役に復帰する」　(l. 9) **transform A into B**「AをBに変える、変身させる」　(l. 12) **convincingly**「もっともらしく、それらしく」　(l. 12) **on the face of it**「見たところ、表面的には」　(l. 15) **greyhound**「グレーハウンド」（エジプト原産の犬の一品種。四肢が長く、体も細い。走力・視力にすぐれ、猟犬・競争犬に用いる）

p. 24

(l. 4) **hyperrealist**「超写実的な、超リアルな」　(l. 4) **historical figure**「歴史上の人物、歴史上の偉人」　(l. 12) *How the Grinch Stole Christmas*『グリンチ』（2000年のロン・ハワード監督作品。ジム・キャリーが特殊メイクでクリスマス嫌いの奇妙な生き物グリンチを演じた）

(l. 13) *The Curious Case of Benjamin Button*『ベンジャミン・バトン：数奇な人生』（2008年のデビッド・フィンチャー監督作品。アカデミー・メイクアップ賞を受賞）　(l. 18) **shorten someone's life**「寿命を縮める」（I'm … shortening は I was … shortening が正しい）

p. 25

(l. 2) **liquid resin**「液状樹脂、液状レジン」　(l. 3) **life cast**「ライフキャスト」（生きている人から直接型取りして作成する像）　(l. 9) **Adam's apple**「喉仏」　(l. 11) **application**「塗ること、塗布、着用」

Judgments to Make

[T / F] 1. In real life Gary Oldman and Winston Churchill look exactly alike.

[T / F] 2. According to Tsuji, Gary Oldman can be compared to a greyhound, whereas Winston Churchill resembles a bulldog.

[T / F] 3. Kazuhiro Tsuji has always been a sculptor.

[T / F] 4. Gary Oldman says he would not have been able to play the role of Churchill without Tsuji's help.

[T / F] 5. Tsuji decided to leave the movie industry because he felt the stress that his work imposed was too much to endure.

[T / F] 6. The six pieces that Tsuji designed for Oldman include a prosthetic Adam's apple.

[T / F] 7. On his own, Tsuji did the job of daily application of his prosthetics for over three hours, every day for almost 50 days.

[T / F] 8. According to Tsuji, what is great about Gary Oldman is that, once the special makeup has been applied, he almost *becomes* Winston Churchill.

 Partial Composition

1. 彼が演技の道半ばで辞めてしまった後、彼女は彼を優しく説得して舞台に戻らせなければなりませんでした。

   After he quit halfway through a performance, _____ onto the stage.

2. 彼の演奏がいかに素晴らしかったとしても、それは過去の彼のコンチェルトでの出来には及びませんでした。

   _____, it did not measure up to some of his past renderings of concertos.

Unit 4

Lukewarm Welcome

　ヨーロッパでは各国が数千人規模で難民を受け入れているが、日本では難民認定されるのは、ほんのひと握り。申請を却下されても一時滞在許可をもらい5年、10年と日本に滞在している人もいるが、彼らはいつ強制退去命令が出されるか不安に怯え、仕事に就くことや町を離れるといった市民生活の基本的な自由もないという。あるクルド人難民一家を取材した。

Warm Up

【聴き取りのポイント】

下線部に注意しながら、聴いてみよう。

1. a. They get temporary <u>permits</u>, renewed every few months.
   b. (They) can't even leave their city without <u>permission</u>.
2. a. About 2,000 ethnic Kurds live in Japan, most seeking <u>refuge</u>.
   b. A strict policy that only gives <u>refugee</u> status to a select few.

ポイント

下線部のアクセントの位置に気をつけながら聴いてみよう。

【内容理解のポイント】

次の文を考えてみよう。

1. He re-applies at the immigration bureau <u>every two months</u>.
2. Japan rejects almost <u>every asylum application</u> it gets.

ポイント

下線部に注意しながら、1. と 2. を和訳しよう。

Words and Phrases to Study

abuse	apply for
asylum	conflict
deport	homogenous
insular	qualify
refugee	take in

Definition

conflict 1. a serious fighting between two or more groups of people or countries due to differences of opinions or interests

_____ 2. to be entitled or have the right to a particular benefit or privilege by fulfilling a necessary condition

_____ 3. the improper use of something, usually a harmful or morally wrong activity

_____ 4. uninterested in anything outside one's own country or group

_____ 5. protection or safety granted by a state for people who left their home country for political reasons

_____ 6. to force someone to leave a country due to an illegal status or for breaking the law

_____ 7. to allow a person to stay in your house, place, or country

_____ 8. alike and of the same kind; consisting of parts or people that are similar to each other

_____ 9. to formally request for something such as a job or membership by writing a letter or filling in a form

_____ 10. a person who has escaped from his own country due to political, religious or economic reasons, or because of war or natural disaster

Examples

1. The _conflict_ between the two Koreas creates a serious issue which, in my view, can be resolved through negotiation and mutual understanding.

2. After 10 years in Japan, immigrants can finally decide to _____ permanent resident status.

3. To qualify as a _____, one has to show evidences of persecution from the home country.

4. Since Canada has accepted 10,000 refugees this year, Japan is being criticized because she has _____ very few refugees; only 28 out of nearly 11,000 applicants.

5. Working two part-time jobs for two different companies will not _____ for health benefits with either one.

6. The United Nations set down rules for countries accepting refugees seeking _____.

7. This is clearly an _____ of the public funds, and I hope citizens rise up against this and take some actions to stop this.

8. According to history, Japan being an island nation was somewhat _____ in accepting influences from the rest of the world.

9. U.S. authorities catch a lot of illegal migrants from all over the world and _____ them back to their countries of origin.

10. The country is for the most part an extremely _____ society, composed of a people who share one language, culture, and history.

クルド人は、かつてオスマン帝国 (Ottoman Empire) の山岳地帯に居住していたが、第一次世界大戦後 (World War I)、西欧列強 (Western great powers) が引いた国境線により、その居住地はトルコ (Turkey)、イラク (Iraq)、イラン (Iran)、シリア (Syria) などの国々に分断された。現在、世界中で約 2500 万～ 3000 万人いると推定されるクルド人は、国を持たない世界最大の民族と呼ばれている。政治的弾圧や不平等な扱いを受け、次第に世界各地に難民として逃れるようになった。

Blanks to Fill in

Fill in the blanks with suitable words.

Anna Coren (Anchor):

Well, some of the people fleeing conflict in the Middle East are seeking safety in Japan. Immigration is a controversial topic there. While the country donates billions of dollars to international refugee programs, it rejects almost every asylum application it gets. Well, CNN's Will Ripley met Kurds living in limbo outside Tokyo.

Will Ripley (Reporter):

A rare taste of Kurdish hospitality in Japan. This family of refugees welcomes us into their home—their home ⁽¹⁾_____ ⁽²⁾_____ ⁽³⁾_____ ⁽⁴⁾_____. About 2,000 ethnic Kurds live in Japan, most seeking refuge from sectarian violence. This family fled the Turkish-Syrian border ⁽⁵⁾_____ ⁽⁶⁾_____ ⁽⁷⁾_____ ⁽⁸⁾_____ ⁽⁹⁾_____.

They've learned Japanese, local customs, and live quietly in a small Kurdish enclave north of Tokyo.

But they don't have a permanent home. Japan can deport them at any time because of a strict policy that only gives refugee status to a select few and leaves everyone else in limbo. Mesut Gul has been living "temporarily" in Japan for 11 years. He re-applies at the immigration bureau every two months. When he tried to re-apply in December, something he's done more than 60 times, immigration workers told him he was being deported, his request for refugee status finally denied. Locked in detention for five months, Gul became seriously ill. Officers (10)_____ (11)_____ (12)_____ (13)_____ (14)_____ in shackles.

Gul is appealing his deportation order. He says even this life (15)_____ (16)_____ (17)_____ what he'd face back home.

Japan's justice ministry says nearly 11,000 people applied for asylum last year, a record. The immigration bureau accepted just 28 refugees. The government tells CNN people abuse the system, that many seeking refugee status are actually economic migrants and that Japan, the world's third-largest economy, already donates billions of dollars to refugee programs.

But this homogenous, insular society (18)_____ (19)_____ (20)_____ (21)_____ take in migrants. Prime Minister Shinzo Abe says Japan needs to focus on restarting its economy (22)_____ (23)_____ (24)_____ (25)_____ its refugee policy.

Unit 4: Lukewarm Welcome 33

Is Japan's immigration system designed to grind people down to make them want to leave?

"From my 35 years of experience in immigration, I would say Japan wants to send them back," says Hidenori Sakanaka. The former head of Tokyo's immigration bureau is trying to change the system. "The time has come (26)_____ (27)_____ (28)_____ (29)_____ more refugees and immigrants," he says.

Not one Turkish Kurd has ever been granted refugee status in Japan. Instead, they get temporary permits, renewed every few months. (30)_____ (31)_____ (32)_____ (33)_____, don't qualify for healthcare and can't even leave their city without permission.

A constant state of uncertainty, even for students like 19-year-old Ramazan Dursun. His parents brought him here as a child.

"I dream about having a future in Japan," he says. "But if I'm deported, everything I learned, everything I built here, will disappear."

In Japan, he and other refugees find (34)_____ (35)_____ (36)_____ (37)_____ (38)_____, their lives, their futures, in limbo.

Will Ripley, CNN, Kawaguchi, Japan.

📝 Notes

(Title) **lukewarm**「熱意がこもっていない、乗り気でない」

p. 32

(l. 2) **flee**「〜から逃げる」　　(l. 2) **the Middle East**「中東」　　(l. 3) **controversial**「論議を呼ぶ、物議を醸す」　　(l. 4) **donate A to B**「A を B に寄付する、提供する」　　(l. 4) **refugee**「難民、避難民、亡命者」　　(l. 5) **asylum application**「亡命申請、難民申請」　　(l. 6) **Kurd**「クルド人」　　(l. 6) **in limbo**「中途半端な状態で、中ぶらりん状態で」　　(l. 9) **home**「1. 家、住居；2. 故国；故郷；3. 心安らかに暮らせる所、安住の地」　　(l. 11) **seek refuge from**「〜からの庇護（ひご）を求める、〜から避難する」　　(l. 11) **sectarian**「派閥の、宗派の、宗派間の」　　(l. 11) **Turkish**「トルコの」　　(l. 14) **enclave**「（少数民族や外国人などの）居留地」

p. 33

(l. 2) **refugee status**「難民という立場、難民認定」　　(l. 2) **a select few**「選ばれた少数、厳選された人たち」　　(l. 4) **re-apply**「再び申し込む、再申請する」　　(l. 4) **immigration bureau**「入国管理局」　　(l. 7) **(be) locked in ~**「〜に閉じ込められている、監禁されている」　　(l. 8) **detention**「拘留、監禁」　　(l. 8) **seriously ill**「重病で、重症で」　　(l. 9) **shackles**「手かせ、足かせ」　　(l. 10) **appeal**「〜を上訴する、控訴する」　　(l. 10) **deportation order**「国外追放命令、国外退去命令」　　(l. 11) **face**「（困難・苦境に）直面する」　　(l. 11) **back home**「故国で」　　(l. 12) **justice ministry**「法務省」　　(l. 15) **economic migrant**「経済移民、出稼ぎ労働者」　　(l. 18) **insular**「島国根性の、閉鎖的な、偏狭な」　　(l. 20) **focus on~**「〜に重点を置く、〜を重要視する」

p. 34

(l. 1) **be designed to do**「〜するように意図されている、作られている」　　(l. 1) **immigration system**「出入国管理制度」　　(l. 1) **grind … down**「（次第に）〜の力をなえさせる」　　(l. 3) **I would say** (that)「〜だと思う、おそらく〜だろう」　　(l. 8) **grant A B**「A に B（権利など）を許可する、与える」　　(l. 9) **temporary permit**「一時的な許可、一時滞在許可証」　　(l. 9) **renew**「〜を更新する、延長する」　　(l. 10) **qualify for**「〜の資格がある、受給資格がある」　　(l. 11) **healthcare**「医療保険、健康保険（= healthcare insurance）」　　(l. 11) **permission**「許可、承諾、承認」　　(l. 12) **constant state of …**「絶え間ない〜の状態、常に〜の状態」

Judgments to Make

[T / F]   1. Due to Japan's high rejection of asylum application, immigration has become a controversial issue there.

[T / F]   2. Hopeful migrants, like the ethnic Kurds have to apply for refugee status every two months at the immigration bureau to continue residing in Japan.

[T / F]   3. Mesut Gul has been denied of refugee status because of a serious illness resulting in detention for five months.

[T / F]   4. In order to stay in Japan, Gul requests the immigration to reconsider its deportation order given to him.

[T / F]   5. After living for more than a decade in Japan, Gul believes that his way of life back home is almost the same as his in Japan.

[T / F]   6. Prime Minister Shinzo Abe believes that the refugee policy must be given attention after restructuring Japan's economy.

[T / F]   7. The former head of Tokyo's immigration bureau agrees with Prime Minister Abe that Japan should wait for the best time to accept more refugees and immigrants.

[T / F]   8. To date, no Turkish Kurd has been granted refugee status in Japan.

Partial Composition

1. 2016年の政府の数字によると、90,000人が引きこもりの生活を送っており、政府はこの社会問題に目を向けるべきです。さもなければ、彼らは宙ぶらりんのまま暮らし続けることになります。

   According to government figures in 2016, there are 900,000 individuals living as *hikikomori* and the Japanese government should pay attention to this social issue. Otherwise, _____.

2. 高額の税金で外国人労働者が萎えてしまい他の国へと移り住んでしまうので、日本は彼らを引き止めるのに苦労しています。

   Japan has a hard time holding foreign workers because its high government _____ to another country.

36   English for the Global Age with CNN, Vol. 20

Unit 5

Otherworldly Genius

　スティーブン・ホーキング博士が、2018年3月14日亡くなった。ホーキング博士は、21歳で筋萎縮性側索硬化症(ALS)と診断され、余命2年と宣告を受けながら、それに屈することなく、76歳まで研究と科学の啓蒙を続けた。ホーキング博士は、理論物理学者としてケンブリッジ大学で教鞭をとり、宇宙の起源やブラックホールの研究などを行った正に宇宙物理学の先覚者である。博士は、人類の存続を常に憂慮していた。博士曰く、「人類破壊の危機は増大しているが、200年以内に、危機を回避できたら、人類は、安全である」。とてつもなく大きくて、遠い話である。

　この章では、博士の人生を簡単に振り返っている。音声合成装置の声を通じて、宇宙の危機を紹介する一方、研究以外で、無重力飛行を体験し、車椅子からの解放を楽しんだり、博士の娘さんと一緒に宇宙に関する児童書を執筆したりしたことを紹介している。また自分の人生が映画化された『スター・トレック』にも出演し、その顧問を務めた。この章は、彼の書物についても触れている。宇宙物理学者として科学の普及に努め、あらゆることに挑戦を続けたホーキング博士は、多くの人に勇気を与えた。

 **Warm Up**

【聴き取りのポイント】

ポイント

Stephen Hawking 博士の声は、自然発話ではなく、音声合成装置によるものである。CNN の記者の語りと比較してみよう。どのような違いが聞き取れるだろうか。

【内容理解のポイント】

次の文を考えてみよう。

1. It (ALS) left him wheelchair-bound…unable to speak on his own.
2. But the disease could do nothing to confine the brilliance of his mind.
3. This rare form of motor neuron disease left him virtually paralyzed.

ポイント

下線の部分に注意し、上の3つの文章を自然な日本語で表現してみよう。

4. By any measure, Stephen Hawking's life was incredible, even more so because in the 1960s, he was diagnosed with ALS, or motor neuron disease, and given just a few years to live.

ポイント

下線の部分を考えてみよう。記者が伝えたいものは何か。（テキストを聴き・読み終えてから、答えること）。

Words and Phrases to Study

> diagnose   species
> physics   nomination
> optimist   depict
> negotiate   profound
> revere   wheelchair

Definition

depict 1. to describe something

_____ 2. to find out what illness someone has

_____ 3. to discuss something in order to reach an agreement, especially in business or politics

_____ 4. an official recommendation of someone or something for an election, a position, a duty or a prize

_____ 5. a person who is inclined to be hopeful and to expect good results

_____ 6. the branch of science that deals with matter, energy, and their interactions

_____ 7. very deep, great or severe

_____ 8. to respect and admire someone or something very much

_____ 9. a group of animals or plants the members of which are similar and can together produce young animals or plants

_____ 10. a chair with wheels designed for use by people who cannot walk

Examples

1. The mud-covered teddy bear _depicts_ the sadness of a little girl lost in the heavy rain.

2. When it came to defeating Belgium in the 2018 World Cup, Japanese soccer fans were _____: they were confident that Japan would win.

3. The author's relationship with his mother produced a _____ influence upon the ways in which he portrayed women in his novels.

4. Haruki Murakami is _____ as one of the best among contemporary Japanese writers.

5. Many kinds of animal, bird, fish and plant of foreign origin are being removed in order to protect Japan's native _____.

6. In spite of the fact Mao Kobayashi was _____ with the cancer that, in 2017, took her life, through the Facebook bloggings that she made during her illness, she gave inspiration to many other people.

7. Newton saw an apple fall, and this gave him an idea of how gravity works. This idea is now a fundamental law of _____.

8. In the Paralympics, competitors in fencing and tennis matches and basketball games use _____.

9. When U.S. President Trump met with North Korea's Kim Jong Un, their agenda was to _____ de-nuclearization and mutual economic development.

10. _____ for Hollywood's Oscar and Emmy awards are the movie and TV industries' biggest events.

スティーブン・ホーキング氏は 21 歳の若さで **ALS (amyotrophic lateral sclerosis)**［筋萎縮性側索硬化症］と診断され、余命 2 年と宣告されている。これは、脳から筋肉への 命令が伝わらなくなり、全身の筋力が弱まり、歩行、嚥下、発話などが困難になる原因不明の難病である。2004 年のインタビューで彼は「21 歳のとき、私の期待値はゼロとなった。その後のすべてはボーナスのようなもの」(**My expectations were reduced to zero when I was 21. Everything since then has been a bonus.**) と語っている。車椅子生活になりながらも、精力的に研究と科学の啓蒙に取り組み、2018 年 3 月 14 日、76 歳で亡くなるまで、多くの人に勇気を与え続けた。

 **Blanks to Fill in**

Fill in the blanks with suitable words.

Amara Walker (Anchor):

Now, for most of his life, [Stephen] Hawking battled ALS, a neurodegenerative disease. It left him wheelchair-bound, paralyzed, and eventually unable to speak on his own. But the disease could do nothing to confine the brilliance of his mind. Senior international correspondent Matthew Chance has a brief history of Stephen Hawking.

Matthew Chance (Reporter):

By any measure, Stephen Hawking's life was incredible, even more so because in the 1960s, he was diagnosed with ALS, or motor neurone disease, and (1)_____ (2)_____ (3)_____ (4)_____ (5)_____ to live. This rare form of motor neuron disease left him virtually paralyzed, unable to express his profound vision of humanity and science without a voice synthesizer.

Stephen Hawking (Physicist):

At one point, I thought I would see the end of physics as we know it. But now, I think the wonder of discovery will continue (6)_____ (7)_____ (8)_____ (9)_____ (10)_____ .

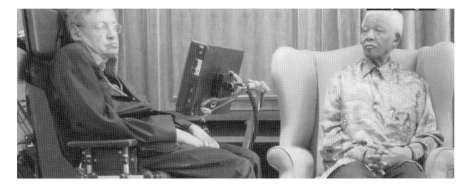

Matthew Chance:

But this was never a man bound by his own physical limitations. He reveled in a zero-gravity flight freeing him, he said, from the confines of his wheelchair. He also wrote ⁽¹¹⁾_____ ⁽¹²⁾_____ ⁽¹³⁾_____ ⁽¹⁴⁾_____ ⁽¹⁵⁾_____ ⁽¹⁶⁾_____ ⁽¹⁷⁾_____ with his daughter Lucy. He had two other children and three grandchildren.

For more than three decades he was a professor at Cambridge University's Department of Applied Mathematics and Theoretical Physics, specializing in the study of black holes and revered ⁽¹⁸⁾_____ ⁽¹⁹⁾_____ ⁽²⁰⁾_____ ⁽²¹⁾_____ ⁽²²⁾_____ ⁽²³⁾_____ ⁽²⁴⁾_____ .

But Professor Hawking also did much to popularize science, playing himself in *Star Trek* and *The Simpsons*. In 2014, his life and romance with wife Jane Wilde was depicted on the big screen in the acclaimed film *The Theory of Everything*.

Hawking consulted on the biodrama, which earned five Academy Award nominations and a Best Actor win for Eddie Redmayne for his portrayal of the physicist.

Hawking's most famous work, *A Brief History of Time*, remains ⁽²⁵⁾_____ ⁽²⁶⁾_____ ⁽²⁷⁾_____ ⁽²⁸⁾_____ ⁽²⁹⁾_____ ⁽³⁰⁾_____ ⁽³¹⁾_____ ⁽³²⁾_____. And he was deeply concerned with humanity's survival.

Stephen Hawking:

I see great danger for the human race. There have been a number of times in the past when its survival has been a question of touch and go. The frequency of such occasions ⁽³³⁾_____ ⁽³⁴⁾_____ ⁽³⁵⁾_____ ⁽³⁶⁾_____ ⁽³⁷⁾_____ ⁽³⁸⁾_____ ⁽³⁹⁾_____. We shall need great care and judgment to ⁽⁴⁰⁾_____ them all successfully. But I'm an optimist. If we can avoid disaster for the next two centuries, our species should be safe as we spread into space.

Matthew Chance:

He was, as ever, looking firmly to the future.

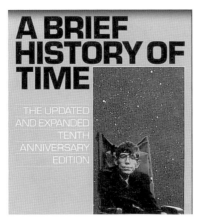

✏️ Notes

(Title) **Otherworldly Genius**「この世のものとは思えない、驚くべき天才」

p. 41

(l. 2) **battle**「〜と戦う（戦争、スポーツ、ゲーム、病気など）」　(l. 2) **ALS** = amyotrophic lateral sclerosis「筋委縮性側策硬化症」　(l. 2) **neurodegenerative disease**「神経変性病、神経変性疾患」　(l. 3) **leave A B**「AをBの状態にする」　(l. 3) **bound**「縛られた」('bind' の過去分詞)　(l. 3) **paralyzed**「麻痺した」('paralyze' の過去分詞)　(l. 5) **confine**「制限する、閉じ込める」　(l. 6) **a brief history of**（ホーキング著の *A Brief History of Time*（邦題『ホーキング、宇宙を語る——ビッグバンからブラックホールまで』）を踏まえて使われていると思われる）　(l. 8) **by any measure**「どう見ても」　(l. 8) **even more so because**「〜だから、なおさら（信じられない）」　(l. 9) **motor neurone disease** = motor neuron disease「運動ニューロン病」（記者はリポートの中で neurone と neuron の両方を使っているが、どちらかに統一するのが適切）　(l. 11) **virtually**「実質上、事実上」　(l. 13) **voice synthesizer**「音声合成装置」

p. 42

(l. 3) **freeing him, … from the confines of his wheelchair**（分詞構文になっている）　(l. 8) **applied mathematics**「応用数学」　(l. 8) **theoretical physics**「理論物理学」　(l. 11) **popularize**「社会に広める、一般化する」（popular（広まっている、人気がある、形容詞））　(l. 12) *Star Trek*『スター・トレック』（1966年に始まったアメリカのSFシリーズ）　(l. 12) *The Simpsons*『ザ・シンプソンズ』（1989年にアメリカで放映が開始されたアニメーション・コメディ）　(l. 13) **was**（主語が2つ (his wife と (his) romance) あり、were となるべき）　(l. 13) **acclaimed**「高く評価された」　(l. 13) *The Theory of Everything*『博士と彼女のセオリー』（ホーキング博士と彼を長年支え続けた元妻ジェーンの半生を描いた、2014年制作のイギリス映画）　(l. 15) **biodrama**「伝記ドラマ」（Bio は生き物の意味（例 biology, biography, bio-data））　(l. 16) **Best Actor win**「主演男優賞受賞」　(l. 17) **portrayal**「描写」

p. 43

(l. 4) **humanity's survival**「人類の生存、存続」　(l. 7) **touch and go**「不安な（危うい）状態」（くだけた表現）　(l. 8) **frequency**「頻度」（frequent（頻繁な、形容詞））　(l. 12) **spread into**「〜に広がる」　(l. 14) **as ever**「相変わらず、いつものように」　(l. 14) **firmly**「しっかりと、断固として」

Judgments to Make

[T / F] 1. Hawking did not lose his ability to speak on his own.

[T / F] 2. The length of his life was exactly as expected.

[T / F] 3. He kept his ability to think and hear to the end of his life.

[T / F] 4. Due to his illness, Hawking worked at Cambridge University for only 10 years.

[T / F] 5. Hawking wanted as many people as possible to learn about the reality of the universe.

[T / F] 6. He showed no interest in TV programs or movies.

[T / F] 7. He was concerned with the question of how much longer the human species will be able to survive.

[T / F] 8. Hawking predicted that the earth will survive for another 200 years.

 Partial Composition

1. 「平成30年7月豪雨」では、約200人近くの人が亡くなり、7,000人の日常生活が麻痺し、避難生活を強いられた。

    "Heavy Rain in July 2018" in Japan _____ dead, and about 7,000 people in shelters, their daily lives paralyzed.

2. 2018年のワールドカップでは、日本チームの3戦目の相手は、ベルギーだった。ゲーム後半の終盤では、いっとき、誰もが2対2の引き分けだと思った。

    In the 2018 World Cup, Japan's 3rd opponent was Belgium. _____ toward the end of the second half, we all thought the Japanese team would tie 2-2.

Unit 6

A Different London Tube

　大英博物館やウェストミンスター宮殿が立ち並ぶロンドン中心部の真下に、総距離37キロの地下トンネル網がある。郵便物の運搬用に作られたもので、昼夜を問わず無人で走り続けていたというが、その存在はほとんど知られてこなかった。75年以上の長きにわたりロンドンの郵便輸送を支えてきた「秘密の通路」が今年、新たな観光名所として生まれ変わった。

 **Warm Up**

【聴き取りのポイント】

下線部に注意しながら、聴いてみよう。

 After 75 years of service, the mail train was shut down in 2003—1,000 tons of cast-iron rail track left to rust.

ポイント

下線部に注意しながら聴いて、実際に発音してみよう。

【内容理解のポイント】

次の文を考えてみよう。

This is a small railway with a proud history: from the beginning, in 1927, operating with the world's first driverless electric trains, up to 4 million letters a day shifting across London to various sorting-offices, part of the great social network of its day: the Royal Mail

ポイント

1. 下線部 "proud history"（「誇高き歴史」）とは何のことか考えよう。
2. レポートのポイントとも言える、この部分を訳してみよう。

Unit 6: A Different London Tube

Words and Phrases to Study

abandon	brand-new
crew	deliver
descend	eerie
haunt	rumble
shut down	the Tube

Definition

descend   1. to move from a higher level to a lower one

_____ 2. to go away from a place, vehicle, etc., permanently, especially because the situation makes it impossible for you to stay

_____ 3. to stop the working of one or more large machines, either temporarily or permanently

_____ 4. to make a long series of low, indistinct sounds, especially as seeming to come from a great distance away

_____ 5. to take goods, letters, packages, etc., to a particular place or person

_____ 6. the train-system that runs under the ground in London

_____ 7. a group of people with special skills that works as a team

_____ 8. new and not yet used

_____ 9. (of a ghost or spirit) to manifest itself at (a place) regularly

_____ 10. strange and slightly frightening

Examples

1. I knew he was upstairs, but then heard his footsteps _descending_ the stairs.

2. We could hear thunder _____ in the distance.

3. I love the London _____: it's affordable, safe, fast and efficient, and it can get you anywhere in London.

4. There's a TV reporter and a film-_____ outside, waiting to interview you.

5. A big tsunami that hit the area resulted in the nearby nuclear power-plant being _____.

6. The flickering of silent lightning can make a summer night seem a little _____.

7. Since the family that owned it suddenly disappeared, this house has remained _____.

8. I suspect this hotel is _____: at three o'clock every morning, I am being woken up by faint sounds of children laughing.

9. The morning mail has just been _____.

10. I prefer to buy old furniture—not shiny, _____ stuff.

英国で郵便事業が始まったのは 1516 年。手紙の配達には、1784 年からは郵便馬車、1830 年からは鉄道が利用されていたが、20 世紀に入ると道路の渋滞や霧のせいでロンドン市内の配達に支障が出始めた。それを解消すべく、地下 21 メートルを走る郵便物運搬専用の鉄道の建設計画が持ち上がり、1927 年、郵便鉄道 (Mail Rail) が開業した。全盛期には毎日 400 万通もの郵便物を 1 日 24 時間運んでいたという。

2003 年、郵便 (email に対して、snail mail (カタツムリのように遅いことから) とも呼ばれる) 利用が減少したことなどにより、その役目を終えたが 2017 年にオープンしたばかりの郵便博物館 (The Postal Museum) のメインアトラクションとして息を吹き返した。2 両編成の観光列車に乗り、約 20 分かけて全長 37 キロの路線の一部を巡る体験ができるそうだ。

 Blanks to Fill in

Fill in the blanks with suitable words.

Max Foster (Anchor):

You might live here in London and never know it's right beneath your feet. For decades, the Royal Mail delivered letters via an underground system that's been abandoned for years. From Tuesday, it'll be the city's newest tourist attraction, though. CNN's Nick Glass takes us for a ride.

Nick Glass (Reporter):

Carefully descending about 25 meters underground to an eerie, subterranean world ⁽¹⁾_____ ⁽²⁾_____ ⁽³⁾_____ ⁽⁴⁾_____ ⁽⁵⁾_____ and fewer have ever seen, a web of miniature tunnels burrowed deep down into the London clay, and spread right across the capital. This is the old British Post Office railway network, two tracks ⁽⁶⁾_____ ⁽⁷⁾_____ ⁽⁸⁾_____ ⁽⁹⁾_____ ⁽¹⁰⁾_____ for 10 extraordinary kilometers.

The men pushing the locomotive are the last of the maintenance crew.

50　English for the Global Age with CNN, Vol. 20

Graham Devitt (Mail Rail Worker):

 We run ⁽¹¹⁾_____ ⁽¹²⁾_____ ⁽¹³⁾_____ ⁽¹⁴⁾_____, and it's amazing that nobody ever knew we were here.

Ray Middlesworth (Mail Rail Worker):

I mean, it's a Tube, half-scale Tube. We talk to other people, and they say it's a bit spooky or a bit eerie, but to us, it's like our front room.

Nick Glass:

But what a front room: a warren of tunnels, most ⁽¹⁵⁾_____ ⁽¹⁶⁾_____ ⁽¹⁷⁾_____ ⁽¹⁸⁾_____ ⁽¹⁹⁾_____, some just two meters. The place feels abandoned, with the deadness of a catacomb. After 75 years of service, the mail train was shut down in 2003—1,000 tons of cast-iron rail track left to rust, and thin-fingered stalactites left dripping from the roof.

This is a small railway with a proud history, from the beginning, in 1927, operating with the world's first driverless electric trains, up to 4 million letters a day shifting across London to various sorting offices, part of the great social network of its day, the Royal Mail.

⁽²⁰⁾_____ ⁽²¹⁾_____ ⁽²²⁾_____ ⁽²³⁾_____ ⁽²⁴⁾_____

⁽²⁵⁾_____—by pickax and shovel—and took over three years to build, rib after cast-iron rib.

The Post Office slogan was "Speed, speed, speed." The trains never stopped, operating (26)_____ (27)_____ (28)_____, 24 hours a day.

Ray Middlesworth has worked down here for 30 years. His wife grew up in central London and, until she met Ray, had always thought her childhood home was haunted: (29)_____ (30)_____ (31)_____ (32)_____ in the basement.

Ray Middlesworth:

1-82
1-87

She told me she lived in Rugby Street, and I thought, 'Our railway goes underneath Rugby Street.' And when I checked the Ordnance Survey map, we went directly underneath their house. So the vibrations and noise they heard in the dead of night were our trains rumbling by underneath.

Nick Glass:

The tunnels have been silent now for 13 years or so. A brand-new, battery-powered train will be back on the tracks down here. And rather than letters, it will carry tourists (33)_____ (34)_____ (35)_____ (36)_____, and be used to help tell the 500-year-old history of the British postal service.

Nick Glass, CNN, underground in London.

✏️ Notes

p. 50

(l. 3) **for decades**「何十年もの間」　　(l. 3) **Royal Mail**「ロイヤルメール」(英連合王国の郵便事業会社)　　(l. 5) **tourist attraction**「観光名所」　　(l. 5) **take ... for a ride**「～を（乗り物）に乗せていく」　　(l. 9) **subterranean**「地下の、地中の」　　(l. 10) **web**「蜘蛛の巣状のもの」　　(l. 10) **burrow A into B**「A（穴など）をBに掘る」　　(l. 11) **the London clay**「ロンドン粘土層」(テムズ川流域の地下に広がる古第三紀新世の地層)　　(l. 11) **spread A across B**「AをBの向こうまで伸ばす」　　(l. 12) **the Post Office**「(英国の) 郵政省」　　(l. 12) **railway network**「鉄道網」　　(l. 15) **maintenance crew**「整備班」

p. 51

(l. 1) **Mail Rail**「(ロンドンの) 郵便鉄道」　　(l. 5) **half-scale**「2分の1縮尺」　　(l. 6) **spooky**「幽霊が出そうな、不気味な」　　(l. 6) **front room**「《英》(住居の正面側の) 居間、応接間」　　(l. 8) **what a ...**「なんて～だろう」　　(l. 8) **warren**「入り組んだ迷路のような場所」　　(l. 10) **deadness**「生気のなさ、死の状態」　　(l. 10) **catacomb**「地下墓地」　　(l. 12) **cast-iron**「鋳鉄製の」　　(l. 12) **leave ... to do**「～が（これから）～するままにする」　　(l. 12) **rust**「さびる」　　(l. 12) **thin-fingered**「細い指のような」　　(l. 12) **stalactite**「鍾乳石」　　(l. 12) **leave ... doing**「～が～しているままにする」　　(l. 14) **proud history**「輝かしい歴史、誇るに足る歴史」　　(l. 15) **driverless**「無人運転の、自動運転の」　　(l. 15) **up to ...**「最大～まで」　　(l. 16) **shift**「移動する、移る」　　(l. 16) **sorting office**「仕分け所」　　(l. 19) **pickax**「つるはし」　　(l. 20) **rib**「(丸天井などを補強する) リブ」

p. 52

(l. 4) **grow up**「育つ、子どもの頃を過ごす」　　(l. 7) **basement**「地階、地下室」　　(l. 10) **underneath**「1. ～の下に　2. 下に、下で」　　(l. 10) **Ordnance Survey**「(英国の) 陸地測量局」(地形図の作成などを行う英国政府の行政機関。日本の国土地理院に相当する)　　(l. 12) **in the dead of night**「真夜中に、深夜に」　　(l. 16) **battery-powered**「バッテリー駆動の、電気駆動式の」　　(l. 16) **rather than ...**「～ではなくて」　　(l. 19) **postal service**「郵便事業」

Judgments to Make

[T / F]   1. Until last year, the Royal Mail was still delivering letters via an underground system.

[T / F]   2. The old British Post Office underground railway-system extends for 10 kilometers.

[T / F]   3. The underground railway-system is exactly like a full-scale London Tube.

[T / F]   4. The small railway, operated with driverless electric trains, transferred up to 4 million letters per day.

[T / F]   5. The long tunnels were dug by mechanical excavator.

[T / F]   6. Londoners never felt vibrations or heard noise as the trains ran beneath their houses, deep underground.

[T / F]   7. After the tunnels have been cleaned up, a brand-new train is going to carry tourists across London, but underground.

[T / F]   8. The British postal service has been functioning for more 500 years.

 Partial Composition

1. さあ、これから船長が私たちを（乗り物での）海中探索へと案内して、生物の多様性を見せてくれますよ。

   Now, the captain is going to _____ to discover all the animal-diversity to be found there.

2. 真夜中に家の中で叫び声が響き渡ったかと思うと、一人の女性が出てきました。

   There was a scream in _____, which echoed through the house, and a woman came running out.

Unit 7

Where France Meets Arabia

　アラブ首長国連邦 (UAE) のアブダビに、フランスのルーブル美術館の別館「ルーブル・アブダビ」がオープンした。アブダビ沖の人工島に建てられた同美術館は海に浮かぶような建築で、ドーム型の天井から差し込む日差しは「光の雨」となって内部に降り注ぎ、幻想的な空間を作り出す、他に類を見ない美術館だ。古代から現代に至るまでの美術品 600 点以上を所蔵し、ゴッホやダ・ヴィンチの傑作を鑑賞することができる。

 **Warm Up**

【聴き取りのポイント】

下線部に注意しながら、聴いてみよう。

 The Louvre Abu Dhabi has over 600 artworks on display, from ancient Egyptian artifacts to Vincent van Gogh, even this portrait by Leonardo da Vinci.

> ポイント

下線部の固有名詞の発音を聴いてみよう。

【内容理解のポイント】

次の文を考えてみよう。

When we have the first visitor entering this museum, he is going to see something of fantastic quality. I think that's what's important

> ポイント

1. 下線部の that が何を指しているか考えよう。
2. その上で、全体を訳してみよう。

Words and Phrases to Study

over the horizon	artifact
beauty	civilization
deal	architect
in the making	jewel
on display	spectacular

Definition

architect 1. someone whose job is to design buildings

_____ 2. very impressive

_____ 3. a valuable stone, such as a diamond

_____ 4. an object such as a tool, weapon, etc., that was made in the past and is historically important

_____ 5. a society that is well organized and developed, especially a particular society in a particular place or at a particular time

_____ 6. (of something) in a public place where people can look at it

_____ 7. taking (... years) to make

_____ 8. likely to happen in the future

_____ 9. a very attractive feature that characterizes something

_____ 10. an agreement or arrangement, especially in business or politics, that helps both sides involved

Examples

1. He's a world-famous _architect_ who has designed sports stadiums for many countries.

2. Movie-director Stanley Kubrick was such a perfectionist that his final movie was several years _____.

3. Children will be thrilled by the sight of a Lego model of the Titanic that is scheduled to be placed _____ in this museum.

4. Their success over the years has already meant steady growth in both business and facility-size, with more growth just _____.

5. London's British Museum has the world's largest collection of ancient Egyptian _____ outside of Egypt.

6. The two countries are expected to sign an intergovernmental _____ concerning construction of an undersea gas pipeline.

7. The _____ of this business model is that it's really easy to scale up.

8. All the guest-rooms of the hotel, which is located on a flank of the Kirishima mountains, command a _____ view of the harbor to the south.

9. The crowns worn by queens and kings at state ceremonies are usually ornamented with large _____, as symbols of both wealth and authority.

10. Archaeologists have unearthed evidence of a prehistoric _____ that flourished along one stretch of the Silk Road.

パリのルーブル美術館初の海外別館「ルーブル・アブダビ」がオープンした。当初は 2012 年完成予定だったが、世界金融危機や石油価格の下落の影響で開館が延期されていた。ルーブル・アブダビでは約 600 点の所蔵作品に加えて、フランスの 13 施設から貸し出された 300 点の美術品を展示。レオナルド・ダ・ヴィンチ作「ミラノの貴婦人の肖像」(*La belle Ferronnière*) やクロード・モネ作「サン・サザール駅」(*Gare Saint-Lazare*) などが鑑賞できる。2017 年 1 月には、絵画として史上最高額となる 4 億 5030 万ドルで落札されたダ・ヴィンチの「サルバトール・ムンディ（救世主）」(*Salvator Mundi*) が同美術館で所蔵されることがわかり、話題となった。

Blanks to Fill in

Fill in the blanks with suitable words.

Amara Walker (Anchor 1):

A Parisian crown jewel is landing on this show's home turf, the shores of Abu Dhabi.

Michael Holmes (Anchor 2):

Yeah. Some 10 years in the making, including a five-year holdup, the Louvre Abu Dhabi is finally swinging its doors open.

Amara Walker:

Right now, it's having its official state opening. This weekend, the public will finally get to enjoy the place. This show's very own Becky Anderson ⁽¹⁾_____ ⁽²⁾_____ ⁽³⁾_____ ⁽⁴⁾_____ ⁽⁵⁾_____ to check out this spectacular new museum.

Becky Anderson (Reporter):

 It's taken 10 years and ⁽⁶⁾_____ ⁽⁷⁾_____ ⁽⁸⁾_____ ⁽⁹⁾_____ dollars, but now, the UAE finally has a world-class museum to call its own: the new Louvre Abu Dhabi, which opens this week.

Why did Abu Dhabi want to bring the Louvre? Why here?

Mohamed Khalifa Al Mubarak (Chairman, Abu Dhabi Tourism and Culture Authority):

We felt that we really wanted to create something for the world. It's a museum ⁽¹⁰⁾_____ ⁽¹¹⁾_____ ⁽¹²⁾_____ ⁽¹³⁾_____. And I think the beauty with this museum is that it will talk to everybody.

Becky Anderson:

⁽¹⁴⁾_____ ⁽¹⁵⁾_____ ⁽¹⁶⁾_____ ⁽¹⁷⁾_____ ⁽¹⁸⁾_____ may just be the building itself, designed by award-winning French architect Jean Nouvel. Its centerpiece steel dome shades the 23 galleries below, creating this so-called rain of light.

Jean Nouvel (Architect):

I wanted to create a museum belonging to this civilization, belonging to this country, belonging to history and geography.

Becky Anderson:

Inside, the Louvre Abu Dhabi has over 600 artworks on display, from ancient Egyptian artifacts to Vincent van Gogh, even this portrait by Leonardo da Vinci, its first appearance ⁽¹⁹⁾_____ ⁽²⁰⁾_____ ⁽²¹⁾_____.

Maya Allison (Chief Curator, New York University Abu Dhabi Art Gallery):

Amassing the collection that the Louvre Abu Dhabi has to this point ⁽²²⁾_____ ⁽²³⁾_____ ⁽²⁴⁾_____ ⁽²⁵⁾_____ ⁽²⁶⁾_____ that they have is remarkable.

Becky Anderson:

The Louvre Abu Dhabi is ⁽²⁷⁾_____ ⁽²⁸⁾_____ ⁽²⁹⁾_____ an intergovernmental deal made between France and the UAE in 2007. The brand name alone sold for an estimated $520 million—on loan for 30 years. But for decision makers here, it's ⁽³⁰⁾_____ ⁽³¹⁾_____ ⁽³²⁾_____ ⁽³³⁾_____.

Mohamed Khalifa Al Mubarak:

We hear remarks ⁽³⁴⁾_____ ⁽³⁵⁾_____ ⁽³⁶⁾_____ ⁽³⁷⁾_____ ⁽³⁸⁾_____. I think, first and foremost, we made sure that when we have the first visitor entering this museum, he is going to see something of fantastic quality. I think that's what's important. But what's the most important thing is culture is here to stay. So the…the winner here is culture.

Becky Anderson:

Next up, they say, are two more museums just over the horizon, including a future Guggenheim.

Becky Anderson, CNN, Abu Dhabi.

Unit 7: Where France Meets Arabia

✏ Notes

p. 59
(l. 2) **Parisian**「パリの、パリ人の」　　(l. 2) **crown jewel**「宝物、至宝、極めて貴重なもの」　　(l. 2) **land on ...**「〜に上陸する、やってくる」　　(l. 2) **home turf**「ホームグラウンド、本拠地」　　(l. 2) **shores**「（海岸線を持つ）国」　　(l. 3) **Abu Dhabi**「アブダビ」（アラブ首長国連邦の首都）　　(l. 5) **some**「およそ、約」　　(l. 5) **holdup**「（進行の）停止、停滞」　　(l. 5) **the Louvre**「ルーブル美術館」　　(l. 6) **swing ... open**「（ドア・門などを）さっと開ける」　　(l. 8) **state**「公式の、政府の」　　(l. 9) **get to do**「〜する機会を得る、〜できるようになる」　　(l. 11) **check out**「《話》〜をよく見る、調べる」　　(l. 14) **the UAE** = the United Arab Emirates「アラブ首長国連邦」　　(l. 15) **call ... one's own**「〜を自分の物と言う、わが物とする」

p. 60
(l. 1) **tourism and culture authority**「観光・文化庁」　　(l. 7) **award-winning**「賞を取った」　　(l. 8) **centerpiece**「中心にあるもの、中心的存在」　　(l. 9) **rain of light**「光の雨」（ドームの隙間から光が差し込む様子を示す表現）　　(l. 18) **curator**「（美術館・博物館の）学芸員」　　(l. 19) **amass**「〜を収集する」　　(l. 19) **to this point**「この時点までに」

p. 61
(l. 3) **intergovernmental**「政府間の」　　(l. 4) **brand name**「ブランド名、商標」（ここでは「ルーブル」という名称を指す）　　(l. 4) **sell for ...**「〜の値段で売れる」　　(l. 4) **estimated**「推定の」　　(l. 4) **(be) on loan**「借り入れている、レンタルしている」　　(l. 8) **remark**「意見、発言」　　(l. 9) **first and foremost**「何よりもまず、何を置いても」　　(l. 9) **make sure that ...**「確実に〜であるようにする」　　(l. 12) **(be) here to stay**「定着している、普及している」　　(l. 12) **winner**「得をするもの、利益を手に入れるもの」　　(l. 15) **next up** (is)「次は〜の番だ」　　(l. 15) **two more museums:**（一つはニューヨーク市にある近代美術館のグッゲンハイム美術館の分館で、もう一つはUAEの歴史について知ることができるシェイクザーイド国立博物館）　　(l. 15) **just over the horizon**「兆しが見えて、近い将来に起きそうな」

Judgments to Make

[T / F] 1. It took some 10 consecutive years to build the Louvre Abu Dhabi.

[T / F] 2. It cost hundreds of millions of dollars to construct the museum.

[T / F] 3. Jean Nouvel, who designed the museum-building, is an award-winning French architect.

[T / F] 4. The artworks that the Louvre Abu Dhabi will display include not only ancient Egyptian artifacts but also at least one work by Vincent van Gogh.

[T / F] 5. The construction of the Louvre Abu Dhabi was made possible by a solitary effort on the part of the UAE.

[T / F] 6. The UAE paid in cash an estimated $520 million to buy the brand name "Louvre" outright.

[T / F] 7. Mr. Mohamed Mubarak says money is less important than the museum's being able to show its visitors something of wonderful quality.

[T / F] 8. The UAE is planning to build two more museums, including a future Guggenheim.

 Partial Composition

1. まず何よりも、あなた個人にふりかかった、想像を絶するほど恐ろしい話を私たちとシェアしてくれてありがとうございます。

   _____, _____ sharing your personal story, which is unimaginably horrifying.

2. SNSはこのまま定着すると多くの人が考えています。

   Many people believe social networking service _____.

Unit 8

Storing It and Sharing It

環境保護意識の高いドイツでは、再生可能エネルギーへの転換が推進されている。最近では、自宅で発電した電力を蓄えておく蓄電池を設置する家庭も増えているという。ある企業が提供する蓄電池システムでは、コミュニティー電力を共有することで、利用者同士で余剰電力を融通し合うことが可能だ。

 **Warm Up**

【聴き取りのポイント】

下線部に注意しながら、聴いてみよう。

 Wind turbines and solar panels are part of the landscape in rural Germany.

> ポイント

下線部の発音に気をつけながら聴いて、自分でも発音してみよう。

【内容理解のポイント】

次の文を考えてみよう。

Germany has long been a renewable-energy champion.

> ポイント

下線部に注意しながら、全体を訳してみよう。

Words and Phrases to Study

> challenge   urban
> storage   residential
> integrate   efficient
> consumption   rural
> renewable   landscape

Definition

challenge   1. something that is difficult to accomplish and therefore tests a person's ability

_____ 2. an act of using energy, food, or materials; (or) the amount used

_____ 3. capable of doing something well and thoroughly, with no waste of time, money or energy

_____ 4. to combine two or more things so that they work together

_____ 5. everything you see when you look out across a large area of land, especially in the country

_____ 6. characterizing something that does not run out as a result of being used, such as wind or solar energy

_____ 7. (of an area of a town) developed to be suitable for living in; consisting of houses, rather than factories or offices

_____ 8. connected with or resembling the countryside

_____ 9. a process or a method of keeping something for later use

_____ 10. connected with, or having the characteristics of, a town or city

Examples

1. Even though he had studied for the entrance-exam for over a year, for him it was still an extremely tough _challenge_ .

2. David was praised by his boss for being very _____ in his work.

3. Namba has one of the highest population-rates among Osaka's various quarters, due to its popularity as a convenient _____ area.

4. Many people consider city-centers unpleasant to live in as _____ areas are often busy and noisy throughout the night.

5. Having been born and raised in a small village, and accustomed only to _____ life, she was terrified at the prospect of having to move to a large city.

6. Reliance on cars will mean that _____ of fossil fuel will become difficult to limit.

7. For us to gain a truly peaceful society, we must bring about full _____ among people of all creeds and ethnic backgrounds.

8. There is hardly a single _____ in Japan that has not been spoiled by badly-designed modern buildings, powerlines, and concrete reinforcements of cliffs and river-courses.

9. Though she and her employees wanted to employ energy gained from _____ resources, doing this proved far more expensive than using conventional sources of energy.

10. Since Christopher no longer had room for most of his old books, he rented a _____-container to keep them in until such time as he might be able to sell them off.

Sonnen は 2010 年にドイツで設立された会社。2013 年に国際化も視野に社名を Sonnenbatterie GmbH に変更し、その後、Sonnen GmbH の名称で活動を続けている。Sonnen 社の蓄電池システムを使えば、消費電力の約 80% は太陽光パネルなどを利用した自家発電で賄える。さらに同社が作った顧客のコミュニティに入れば、足りない分の 20% を別の顧客から融通してもらえるので、100% 再生可能エネルギーで電力が賄えるという。太陽光パネルを設置できない都市部の家庭も、蓄電池を購入してコミュニティーに入ることができる。ちなみに同社の蓄電池は、充放電の繰り返しに耐えられるソニー社の製品だそうである。

Blanks to Fill in

Fill in the blanks with suitable words.

Kristie Lu Stout (Anchor):

Many countries are looking at ways to better develop renewable energy sources, and in Germany, a tech company is creating a battery that would let homeowners store renewable energy to power their homes. Isa Soares has this look.

Isa Soares (Reporter):

Wind turbines and solar panels are part of the landscape in rural Germany. The country has long been a renewable-energy champion, but efficient storage for 24-hour use has been a challenge. Tech company Sonnen are combining a battery with community spirit ⁽¹⁾_____ ⁽²⁾_____ ⁽³⁾_____ ⁽⁴⁾_____.

Christoph Ostermann (CEO, Sonnen):

Our battery systems can be ⁽⁵⁾_____ ⁽⁶⁾_____ ⁽⁷⁾_____ ⁽⁸⁾_____ ⁽⁹⁾_____ power generation. So, we are using a very specific cell chemistry, which is called lithium iron phosphate, and we have 20 years calendric lifetime, and our batteries ha...can perform easily 10,000 cycles.

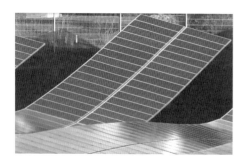

Isa Soares:

If the technology sounds familiar, it's because tech giants like Tesla and Hyundai have (10)_____ (11)_____ (12)_____ (13)_____ lithium-battery installations in the world, switched on and working in Australia and South Korea. The Sonnen system is typically used in residential settings.

Christoph Ostermann:

Tesla has announced to go also into the residential-storage segment, and this helped (14)_____ (15)_____ (16)_____ (17)_____ (18)_____ more attention and awareness.

Isa Soares:

The company's battery system also connects users to a virtual power plant called the sonnenCommunity, where members share their excess energy with others, even if they don't generate their own renewable power.

Christoph Ostermann:

This means that they are (19)_____ (20)_____ (21)_____ (22)_____ cover something like 70, 75 percent of their power consumption with self-consumption; they are able to be 100 percent independent from the tra…traditional utility (23)_____ (24)_____ (25)_____ (26)_____ (27)_____ with…with grid power.

Isa Soares:

There are 30,000 Sonnen users worldwide, with 75 percent distributed in Germany, servicing rural and urban areas alike.

Here in Munich, six months ago, Lars Reubekeul invested in a Sonnen battery for his home.

Lars Reubekeul (sonnenCommunity Member)**:**

I was immediately interested in the…the whole system. (28)_____ (29)_____ (30)_____ (31)_____ is, actually, saving [the] environment—you produce your own electricity on the roof. But at the end of the day, it saves money.

Isa Soares:

Community members can monitor their clean-power production and consumption through an app.

Lars Reubekeul:

I can see the actual consumption of certain equipment in the house, and (32)_____ (33)_____ (34)_____ (35)_____ (36)_____ what is going on and what…what might be changed in the future.

Isa Soares:

Battery-grid technology is maturing, and small-scale community systems are part of the puzzle when it comes to integrating more renewable energy into the global power mix.

Isa Soares, CNN.

✏️ Notes

p. 68
(l. 2) **look at...**「～を考察する、検討する」　(l. 2) **renewable energy source**「再生可能エネルギー源」　(l. 4) **homeowner**「住宅所有者」　(l. 4) **store**「～を蓄える、蓄積する」　(l. 8) **champion**「擁護者、推進派、支持者」　(l. 10) **combine A with B**「A を B と結びつける」　(l. 10) **community spirit**「共同体意識」　(l. 14) **power generation**「発電」　(l. 15) **cell chemistry**「電池化学、電池の化学的性質」　(l. 15) **lithium iron phosphate**「リン酸鉄リチウム」　(l. 16) **calendric**「時間の測定に関する、時間で表す、年数で考える」　(l. 16) **lifetime**「(物の) 寿命、耐用期間」　(l. 16) **easily**「《数量表現の前で》少なくとも、優に」

p. 69
(l. 2) **sound familiar**「(主語に) 聞き覚えがある」　(l. 2) **giant**「大企業」　(l. 2) **Tesla**「テスラ」(アメリカを拠点に 電気自動車・蓄電システムなどの製造販売を行う大手企業)　(l. 3) **Hyundai**「現代グループ、ヒュンダイ」(韓国の巨大企業グループ)　(l. 4) **lithium-battery**「リチウム電池」(ここではハイフンをつけて形容詞として使われている)　(l. 4) **installation**「施設、設備、装置」　(l. 5) **typically**「通常は、主として」　(l. 8) **go into …**「～に参加する、参入する」　(l. 8) **segment**「区分、部門、分野」　(l. 13) **share A with B**「A を B と分け合う」　(l. 13) **excess**「余分な、超過した」　(l. 14) **generate**「～を生み出す」　(l. 18) **cover**「～を賄う」　(l. 18) **something like**「およそ、約」　(l. 18) **power consumption**「電力消費量、消費電力」　(l. 19) **self-consumption**「(電力などの) 自己消費」　(l. 19) **be independent from …**「～ から独立している、～に依存していない」　(l. 20) **utility**「(電気・水道などの) 公共事業(体)」　(l. 21) **grid power**「系統電力」(送電網を通して供給される電力。ここではコミュニティー内でやり取りする電力)

p. 70
(l. 2) **(be) distributed in …**「～に分布している」　(l. 4) **Munich**「ミュンヘン」　(l. 4) **invest in …**「～を買う」　(l. 9) **at the end of the day**「最終的に、結局」　(l. 13) **app**「アプリ」　(l. 17) **go on**「起こる、行われる」　(l. 19) **battery-grid**「蓄電池の電力網の」　(l. 20) **part of the puzzle**「パズルのワンピース、問題解決への鍵の一つ」　(l. 20) **when it comes to …**「～ということになれば」　(l. 21) **power mix**「電力供給構成」

Judgments to Make

[T / F] 1. A tech company in Germany is trying to create a battery that will let people store renewable energy for use in powering their homes.

[T / F] 2. Germany is a country known for its poor use of renewable energy.

[T / F] 3. According to Mr. Ostermann, the batteries that his company is creating can be used for all types of energy-generation.

[T / F] 4. This battery system can also connect users to a virtual power-plant called the sonnenCommunity.

[T / F] 5. While people can cover about seventy five percent of their energy use with this battery, they will not be able to cover one hundred percent.

[T / F] 6. According to Mr. Reubekeul, the main motivation for adoting use of such a battery is to save the environment by producing and storing your own energy.

[T / F] 7. People who use this battery can monitor their power use through an app.

[T / F] 8. Battery-grid systems are not changing and are actually delaying the integration of renewable energy into general energy-production and use.

 Partial Composition

1. その機関は、2020年の国勢調査に先立ち、データベースをよりよく開発する方法を模索しています。

   The organization is _____ in anticipation of the 2020 census.

2. 移民をその土地のコミュニティーに融和させるとなると、鍵を握るのは友情関係である。

   When it _____ the local community, friendship is the key.

Unit 9

Dutch Ingenuity

　オランダは the Netherlands と呼ばれるが、Netherlands は「低い土地」を意味する。その名の通り、国土の約4分の1が海面下（海抜ゼロメートル以下）にあるため、オランダは何世紀もの間、大規模な水害に見舞われてきた。そして1953年の大洪水を機に、同国政府は洪水対策を見直し、堤防やダムの再建・強化に乗り出した。同時に、身近な場所での小さな工夫によっても洪水の危機に対処している。

 **Warm Up**

【聴き取りのポイント】

下線部に注意しながら、聴いてみよう。

1. Much of the country lies below sea <u>level</u>.
2. Frans van de Ven is an urban-water-<u>management</u> expert.
3. The key, he says, is to plan for flooding in comprehensive and <u>multifunctional</u> ways.

ポイント

下線部の発音について、日本語の「レベル」、「マネージメント」、「マルチファンクショナル」と比べて、どう違うか聴いてみよう。

【内容理解のポイント】

次の文を考えてみよう。

<u>By 1987</u>$_{(1)}$, the decision was made to build a movable sea barrier by <u>the busy port of Rotterdam</u>$_{(2)}$.

ポイント

1. 下線部 (1) の意味を考えよう。
2. 下線部 (2) の意味を考えよう。

Words and Phrases to Study

```
flood        sewer
prospect     expert
canal        threat
defend       reservoir
disaster     innovation
```

Definition

canal	1.	a man-made waterway created to allow boats to travel inland
_____	2.	an accident or event that causes great damage and/or loss of life
_____	3.	to do something in order to protect someone or something from being attacked
_____	4.	a person who is extremely skilled in a specific area
_____	5.	an event during which a river or lake overflows its banks and covers an area in unwanted water, usually due to heavy rain
_____	6.	a new idea or invention that is usually intended to improve something that already exists or is done
_____	7.	a possibility of something happening in the future
_____	8.	a large lake the contents of which are used as a water-supply
_____	9.	an underground drainage-system that functions solely so as to remove unwanted water and liquid-waste
_____	10.	a person or thing that is likely to cause damage

Examples

1. A _canal_ was dug, to allow boats to carry coal from the mines down to the nearest sea-port.

2. It has been raining so much, the news said, that we should be prepared for a _____ during the next few days.

3. Japan is famous as a country subject to many different kinds of natural _____, including earthquakes, volcanic eruptions and _tsunami_.

4. After watching TV news-reports of earthquake-damage caused in a neighboring prefecture, the _____ of another earthquake happening closer to home scared him a lot.

5. An efficient _____-system has to be able to deal with everything that people thoughtlessly flush down the toilet, instead of disposing of it as trash that can be burned.

6. Sam had strong ideological beliefs about the need to _____ democracy against fascism.

7. The drought had lasted so long that the local _____ could no longer supply our area with enough water with which to carry on normal life.

8. John is considered an _____ cameraman by many in the movie-industry.

9. Although Rob's dog was large and strong, it was so gentle that it presented nobody with any _____.

10. The invention of the wheel is commonly thought to be the most important _____ in human history.

レポートにも言及があるように、1953年2月1日、暴風雨がオランダ南西部を襲い、4.5メートル以上の高潮が発生。1,835人が亡くなるという同国史上最悪の洪水が起きた。これを受けて1958年、政府は治水対策として、主要な港湾に通じる水路以外の三角州地帯の河口部をすべて塞ぐ「デルタ計画」(The Delta Project) を立案。防潮堤 (storm surge barrier)、水門、可動堰などを設ける大工事を始めた。1997年に可動式のマエスラント堰 (The Maeslant Barrier) が完成し、同計画は完了した。

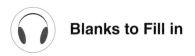 **Blanks to Fill in**

Fill in the blanks with suitable words.

Kristie Lu Stout (Anchor):

 For a country that mostly lies below sea level, the prospect of rising oceans and climate change is serious. But the Netherlands is combining centuries of knowledge with new innovation to help prepare for the future. Matt Rivers has more.

Matt Rivers (Reporter):

 There's a saying in the Netherlands: "God created the earth, but the Dutch created the Netherlands." This nation of 17 million people sits (1)_____ (2)_____ (3)_____ (4)_____ three major rivers, and much of the country lies below sea level. For centuries, the Dutch have (5)_____ (6)_____ (7)_____ (8)_____ (9)_____ from the water.

Marc Walraven (Founder, I-Storm):

We founded this country by making land of it, by dredging the water out of it. But '53 was really the moment that the Dutch government decided we won't have this anymore.

Unit 9: Dutch Ingenuity

Matt Rivers:

That's Marc Walraven, an expert in storm-surge barriers. He's referring to the great flood of 1953. That disaster killed more than 1,800 people (10)_____ (11)_____ (12)_____ (13)_____ overhaul of the nation's flood defenses. Dikes and dams were rebuilt and reinforced.

But by 1987, the decision was made to build a movable sea barrier by the busy port of Rotterdam. Those fully-automated white gates rarely close but early this January, they shut in a heavy storm for the first time in 10 years.

Marc Walraven:

It really touches the Dutch people, 'cause this is (14)_____ (15)_____ (16)_____ (17)_____ (18)_____. And [it's] very visual when we close the Maeslant Barrier, so a lot of people come over here and watch it from the hill and watch it from all locations, so that's… that's pretty nice to see.

Matt Rivers:

People come from all over the world to learn water management from the Dutch. (19)_____ (20)_____ (21)_____ (22)_____ (23)_____ (24)_____ as large as the Maeslant Barrier. Smaller innovations, like this floating park and pavilion, also help the Dutch deal with the danger of flooding.

Frans van de Ven (Urban Land and Water Management Team, Deltares):

The Netherlands is what we say, and I think it's true: it's the safest delta in the world. The flood-protection levels we use here are way beyond flood-protection levels that are ⁽²⁵⁾_____ ⁽²⁶⁾_____ ⁽²⁷⁾_____ in the world.

Matt Rivers:

Frans van de Ven is an urban-water-management expert. The key, he says, is to plan for flooding in comprehensive and multifunctional ways.

This basketball court, for example, ⁽²⁸⁾_____ ⁽²⁹⁾_____ ⁽³⁰⁾_____ ⁽³¹⁾_____ when it storms and then slowly release it into a nearby canal. Similarly, this car park was designed to also serve as a reservoir. It can collect 10 million liters during a downpour, taking pressure off the sewer system. And even these seemingly simple sidewalk tiles can help catch rain.

Frans van de Ven:

In the past, we...we tended to push the water away, only protecting ourselves from the water, but nowadays, ⁽³²⁾_____ ⁽³³⁾_____ ⁽³⁴⁾_____ ⁽³⁵⁾_____ ⁽³⁶⁾_____ ⁽³⁷⁾_____, and...and living with water is pleasant and brings benefits rather than threats.

✐ Notes

(Title) **ingenuity**「創意工夫」

p. 77
(l. 2) **lie**「位置する」　　(l. 2) **below sea level**「海面下に、海抜ゼロメートル以下に」　　(l. 2) **rising oceans**「海面上昇」　　(l. 3) **climate change**「気候変動」　　(l. 3) **combine A with B**「A と B を組み合わせる」　　(l. 7) **saying**「ことわざ、言い習わし」　　(l. 8) **Dutch**「1.《the~》《集合的》オランダ人、オランダ国民；2. オランダの」　　(l. 8) **sit**「位置する、ある」　　(l. 13) **I-Storm** = International Network for Storm Surge Barriers（storm surge barrier「高潮堤、防潮」）　　(l. 14) **found**「～を創設する、建設する」　　(l. 14) **make A of B**「B を A にする、変える」　　(l. 14) **dredge**「～を浚渫（しゅんせつ）する」（drain（水を抜く）の言い間違いと考えられる）　　(l. 15) **'53** = 1953　　(l. 15) **moment**「（重要な）機会、節目」　　(l. 16) **have**「《通例 won't や can't の後に置いて》～を許す、我慢する」

p. 78
(l. 2) **refer to ...**「～に触れる、言及する」　　(l. 4) **overhaul**「（全面的な）見直し、整備」　　(l. 5) **dike**「堤防、土手」　　(l. 5) **reinforce**「～を補強する、強化する」　　(l. 6) **movable**「動かせる、可動式の」　　(l. 7) **busy**「活気のある」　　(l. 7) **Rotterdam**「ロッテルダム」（オランダの南ホラント州にある、世界屈指の港湾都市）　　(l. 11) **touch**「～を感動させる、～の心を動かす」　　(l. 11) **'cause** = because　　(l. 17) **water management**「水管理」　　(l. 20) **deal with ...**「～に対処する」

p. 79
(l. 2) **delta**「三角州、デルタ」　　(l. 3) **way beyond ...**「～をはるかに超えて」　　(l. 8) **comprehensive**「包括的な」　　(l. 8) **multifunctional**「多機能の」　　(l. 10) **release A into B**「A を B に放つ、放出する」　　(l. 11) **serve as ...**「～の機能を果たす、～として役立つ」　　(l. 12) **downpour**「土砂降り」　　(l. 12) **take pressure off ...**「～の負担を軽くする」　　(l. 13) **seemingly**「一見したところ」　　(l. 13) **sidewalk tile**「歩道のタイル」

Judgments to Make

[T / F] 1. The greater part of the Netherlands lies below sea-level.

[T / F] 2. According to what Walraven really wished to say, the Netherlands was created by ridding that greater part of the seawater that once covered it.

[T / F] 3. Although there was, in 1953, a massive flood in the Netherlands, nobody was killed.

[T / F] 4. In 1987, the decision was made to build a large, movable sea barrier across the mouth to Rotterdam port.

[T / F] 5. According to Walraven, since most Dutch people are touched by the Maeslant Barrier, when it was being closed, a lot of them assembled to watch it from nearby.

[T / F] 6. A large number of people travel from all around the world in order to learn water-management-techniques from the Dutch.

[T / F] 7. Frans van de Ven says that the Netherlands is the most dangerous delta in the world because the flood-protection levels are extremely low.

[T / F] 8. Van de Ven thinks that water is very dangerous and that living with it has many disadvantages.

 Partial Composition

1. 20年ぶりに偶然彼女に出会ったけれども、当時と変わらず美しかった。

   I happened _____, but she looked as beautiful as she had been back then.

2. このハンドブックは、これからボランティア・プログラムに参加しようと思っている学生たちのためにガイドとして役立つように作られています。

   This handbook is _____ wishing to participate in a volunteering program.

Unit 10

Putin's Soft Spot

　ロシアのプーチン大統領といえば、泣く子もだまる元KGB捜査官で、2000年5月に大統領就任以来、首相在任期間も含め実質的に18年間、大国ロシアを率いてきた最強の指導者だ。だがその彼も、無条件に相好を崩すときがある。それは動物、特に犬と触れ合うときだ。強面（こわもて）政治家のソフトな一面を紹介する。

 **Warm Up**

【聴き取りのポイント】

下線部に注意しながら、聴いてみよう。

 <u>Russian president Vladimir Putin</u>'s macho persona may have taken a bit of a hit when <u>Turkmenistan</u>'s president gave him a puppy as a belated birthday gift.

● ポイント

下線部の固有名詞に注意しながら聴いてみよう。

【内容理解のポイント】

次の文を考えてみよう。

1. <u>The Russian alpha dog</u> has a history of mixing politics with pooches.
2. While the Russian president may be a former KGB agent with a reputation as a tough guy, he's often <u>revealed his softer side</u> in a long and sometimes illustrious relationship with the animal kingdom.

● ポイント

1. 下線部の the Russian alpha dog とは、誰のもしくは何のことを言っているのだろうか？
2. 下線部は、プーチン大統領のどういう側面を示しているだろうか？

Unit 10: Putin's Soft Spot

Words and Phrases to Study

```
reputation      macho
endangered      migration
tactic          cuddly
flock           reveal
belated         illustrious
```

Definition

belated 1. coming or happening later than should have been the case

_____ 2. having the gentle or appealing quality of a thing or person that you would like to hug

_____ 3. (of animals or plants) having become very rare and in danger of becoming extinct

_____ 4. a group of birds, animals, and even tourists moving together

_____ 5. being admired and respected very much because of what they have achieved

_____ 6. having or showing qualities such as strength and aggression that are in line with traditional ideals about what men should be like

_____ 7. the act of moving from one country or place to live or work in another

_____ 8. a good or bad opinion that people have about someone or something

_____ 9. to show something clearly, or to make something that was not obvious able to be seen

_____ 10. an action or method that is planned in order to achieve a particular goal

84   English for the Global Age with CNN, Vol. 20

Examples

1. She received _belated_ recognition for her groundbreaking work in cancer research.
2. The whales _____ thousands of miles between their feeding ground in the north and their breeding ground in southern seas.
3. After an _____ military career, the general retired and took up fishing.
4. The company broke into the toy market with its _____ series of teddy bears.
5. The young detective learned an effective _____ for solving crimes on a popular television police drama.
6. Two more types of rare birds have been added to the _____ species list.
7. It is difficult for women coaches or referees to be fully accepted in the _____ world of football.
8. The shocked expression on his face _____ exactly how he really felt.
9. It's easy to spot _____ of geese as they migrate.
10. He established a _____ as a first-class playwright with the success of his latest work.

　2017年10月、満面の笑みで子犬の首根っこをつかんで掲げるトルクメニスタンのベルディムハメドフ大統領と、それをにらむようなロシアのプーチン大統領の写真が、ネットをにぎわせた。プーチン氏は、どうやらベルディムハメドフ氏の持ち方が気に入らなかったらしく、子犬を抱き取ったとたんに相好を崩した。東日本大震災後に、復興支援へのお礼として東北地方から贈られた秋田犬も、「ゆめ」と名付けられてかわいがられているようで、2016年冬にもプーチン氏の来日前記者会見に同席して元気な姿を見せた。ちなみに「ゆめ」の返礼として、ロシアからはシベリア猫の「ミール」（ロシア語で「平和」を意味する）が日本に贈られている。

 **Blanks to Fill in**

Fill in the blanks with suitable words.

Michael Holmes (Anchor 1):

 Russian president Vladimir Putin's macho persona may have taken a bit of a hit when Turkmenistan's president gave him a puppy as a belated birthday gift.

Amara Walker (Anchor 2):

Mr. Putin was all smiles, though, as he held the puppy he now calls Verny, which means 'faithful' in Russian.

Amara Walker (Reporter):

 When (1)_____ (2)_____ (3)_____ (4)_____ the Russian president, ordinary tactics might not work on the notoriously fierce leader. But if you bring a puppy, Vladimir Putin's heart might just melt. The Turkmen leader gifted Putin a top-breed pup during their meeting Wednesday. Both men seemed all smiles while Putin held the belated birthday present and posed for a photo op.

If you know Putin, you know this was a smart move. The Russian alpha dog has a history of mixing politics with pooches. Whether it's the Japanese prime minister for a summit in Sochi; or the former Italian prime minister ⁽⁵⁾_____ ⁽⁶⁾_____ ⁽⁷⁾_____ ⁽⁸⁾_____ ⁽⁹⁾_____; or in a meeting with Tony Blair outside Moscow; or having a former U.S. president wait ⁽¹⁰⁾_____ ⁽¹¹⁾_____ ⁽¹²⁾_____ ⁽¹³⁾_____ ⁽¹⁴⁾_____ ⁽¹⁵⁾_____; or even racquetball with the Russian prime minister, you can't hang with Putin if you don't like his dogs.

He made that abundantly clear in a 2007 press conference with the German chancellor Angela Merkel. Merkel, who ⁽¹⁶⁾_____ ⁽¹⁷⁾_____ ⁽¹⁸⁾_____ ⁽¹⁹⁾_____ ⁽²⁰⁾_____ dogs, was photographed looking ⁽²¹⁾_____ ⁽²²⁾_____ ⁽²³⁾_____ Putin's Labrador, and Putin distinctly seemed to not care.

While the Russian president may be a former KGB agent with a reputation ⁽²⁴⁾_____ ⁽²⁵⁾_____ ⁽²⁶⁾_____ ⁽²⁷⁾_____, he's often revealed his softer side in a long and sometimes illustrious relationship with the animal kingdom. ⁽²⁸⁾_____ ⁽²⁹⁾_____ ⁽³⁰⁾_____ ⁽³¹⁾_____ walrus, throwing treats to dolphins at the zoo, [and] feeding baby elk at a Russian national park are among his most cuddly photo ops.

And that's him in 2012 leading a flock of Siberian white cranes to safety in a hang glider. Putin helped the endangered birds prepare for migration in what was dubbed the, quote, "flight of hope." He's also ____(32)____ ____(33)____ ____(34)____ ____(35)____ ____(36)____ tiger, who he received on his 56th birthday, and has personally helped oversee the care of endangered tigers in Siberia.

Before you get all choked up, don't forget Putin is a hunter and a man's man who rides shirtless through the Russian countryside.

📝 Notes

(Title) **soft spot**「（大好きなために）弱いところ、弱み」

p. 86

(l. 2) **persona**「仮面、ペルソナ」　　(l. 2) **take a hit**「打撃を受ける」　　(l. 2) **a bit of …**「ちょっとした〜」　　(l. 3) **Turkmenistan**「トルクメニスタン」（カスピ海の東に位置する共和国。旧ソ連領）　　(l. 3) **puppy**「子犬」　　(l. 6) **be all smiles**「満面の笑みを浮かべている」　　(l. 6) **though**「《話》《文中や文末に置き、軽く付け足して》まあ〜だけどね」　　(l. 10) **work on …**「〜に効果がある、奏功する」　　(l. 10) **notoriously**「悪名高くも」　　(l. 10) **fierce**「荒々しい、こわもての」　　(l. 11) **one's heart melts**「心が和む」　　(l. 12) **Turkmen**「トルクメニスタン人の、トルクメニスタンの」　　(l. 12) **breed**「品種、血統」　　(l. 12) **pup** = puppy「子犬」　　(l. 14) **photo op** = photo opportunity「写真撮影の機会・場面」

p. 87

(l. 1) **move**「戦術、手段」　　(l. 1) **alpha dog**「指導者、最高実力者」　　(l. 2) **have a history of …**「〜の経歴がある、過去がある」　　(l. 2) **mix A with B**「AをBと絡める」　　(l. 2) **pooch**「《話》犬、わんちゃん」　　(l. 5) **have … do**「〜に〜してもらう」　　(l. 7) **racquetball**「ラケットボール」（言い間違いで、実際はバドミントン）　　(l. 8) **hang with …**「〜と親しく付き合う」　　(l. 10) **make … abundantly clear**「〜をきわめて明確にする」　　(l. 10) **press conference**「記者会見」　　(l. 11) **chancellor**「（ドイツなどの）首相」　　(l. 13) **Labrador**「ラブラドール（・レトリーバー）」（カナダのラブラドール半島原産の犬種。賢くて人懐こく、盲導犬や警察犬や猟犬として活躍している）　　(l. 14) **care**「1.《not care》意に介さない、気にしない　2. 世話、保護」　　(l. 15) **KGB**「ソ連国家保安委員会」（旧ソ連の情報機関兼秘密警察。1991年のソ連崩壊に伴って解体し、現在のロシア連邦保安庁などいくつかの組織に権限を移行した）　　(l. 15) **agent**「スパイ、諜報（ちょうほう）員」　　(l. 17) **softer side**「穏やかな側面、優しい面」　　(l. 18) **the animal kingdom**「動物界」　　(l. 19) **walrus**「セイウチ」　　(l. 19) **treat**「おやつ」　　(l. 20) **elk**「ヘラジカ、エルク」

p. 88

(l. 1) **Siberian white crane**「ソデグロヅル」　　(l. 2) **hang glider**（実際は、超軽量飛行機）　　(l. 3) **dub A B**「AにBと名付ける、愛称を付ける」　　(l. 3) **quote**「以下引用」　　(l. 5) **oversee**「〜を監視する、監督する」　　(l. 6) **tigers in Siberia**（アムールトラ（シベリアトラとも）のこと）

Judgments to Make

[T / F] 1. The Japanese prime minister, the former Italian prime minister, Tony Blair, and a former U.S. president also gave Putin a dog.

[T / F] 2. The German chancellor, Angela Merkel, is known to love dogs as much as Putin.

[T / F] 3. Putin enjoys taking photographs of various animals such as elks and dolphins.

[T / F] 4. The present given to Putin by the Turkmen leader was presented to him after Putin's birthday.

[T / F] 5. Putin brings his dogs when he plays racquetball with the Russian prime minister.

[T / F] 6. The so-called "flight of hope" involved Putin flying a hang glider as he escorted endangered birds.

[T / F] 7. Putin likes animals so much that he likes to take his shirt off when he rides horses.

[T / F] 8. Although no numbers are mentioned in the article, it is implied that Putin has other dogs in addition to his Labrador and Verny.

 Partial Composition

1. アリソンさんは仕事の残業や家族の問題でこの一週間は大変だったと聞いていますが、今日の昼過ぎに会ったときは喜色満面のように見えました。

   I know Allison had a rough week with overtime at work and problems at home, but _____ when I saw her today after lunch.

2. 父の葬儀で挽歌を捧げようと思ったのですが、感動で胸がいっぱいになって、最終的に言葉が詰まってしまいました。

   I thought I would be able to give the eulogy at my father's funeral, but _____ that, in the end, I couldn't get the words out.

Unit 11

Neither One nor the Other

　2017年7月1日、中国返還から20年を迎えた香港。特別行政区である香港は「一国二制度」の下、返還から50年間はイギリス統治下のときと同様に、自治が認められることになっており、今のところ、司法の独立や資本主義経済体制を維持している。しかし、2014年には民主化を要求する「雨傘運動」が行われるなど、中国政府による統制強化に懸念が広がっている。

Warm Up

【聴き取りのポイント】

下線部に注意しながら、聴いてみよう。

 Will Hong Kong be <u>allowed</u> to mostly run its own affairs?

◆ ポイント

下線部をよく聴きながら、全体を発音してみよう。

【内容理解のポイント】

次の文を考えてみよう。

1. It's a Special Administrative Region, <u>three words</u> that distinguish it and Macao from the rest of the country.

2. <u>Hong Kong, Inc.</u> has prospered along with the rise of China.

◆ ポイント

1. 下線部が何を指しているかを考えながら、全体を和訳してみよう。
2. なぜ下線部のような言い方をしているのか考えてみよう。

Words and Phrases to Study

> expire paralyze
> liberty momentous
> simultaneously critic
> currency thrive
> anniversary conflict

Definition

anniversary 1. the date on which a significant event took place

_____ 2. a serious disagreement or argument

_____ 3. a person who expresses a negative opinion of something

_____ 4. the system of money used in a country

_____ 5. (of a document or an agreement) to come to the end of its established period of validity

_____ 6. the state of being free, within a society, from oppression

_____ 7. of great importance or significance

_____ 8. make … unable to move

_____ 9. at the same time

_____ 10. to show proper growth or development; to prosper

Examples

1. Steven couldn't believe it was already the 30ᵗʰ _anniversary_ of his wedding.

2. When he saw the spider on his bed, he became _____ by fear.

3. In America, the issue of gun-control is a cause of great _____.

4. The discovery of penicillin was one of the most _____ advances ever made in the field of medicine.

5. Though many people loved the movie, the _____ were all very harsh about it.

6. The climax to that movie had audiences _____ laughing and crying.

7. I've just discovered that I can't come abroad with you—because my passport has just _____.

8. While the chief unit of _____ in continental Europe is the euro, the U.K. uses the pound sterling.

9. Pigeons and crows _____ in cities because they are able to feed on the plentiful food-waste they find there.

10. She was glad she lived in a society that greatly valued personal _____.

雨傘運動 (The Umbrella Movement) は、その名の通り、香港の民主化を求める若者が、武装警察に対する「受け身」の反対を象徴するものとして雨傘を使ったことに由来する。この運動は、全国人民代表大会常務委員会 (the Standing Committee of the National People's Congress (NPCSC)) が、香港の行政長官行政長官 (Hong Kong's chief executive) 候補は指名委員会の過半数の支持が必要であり、候補は2–3人に限定すると決定したことに反発したもの。香港大学の調査によると、18～29歳の若者で「自分は広義の中国人」と答えたのは、わずか3.1%で、「自分は広義の香港人」と答えたのは93.7%で、自分は中国人ではないと考える若者の割合は過去最高となっている。レポートにもあるように、香港人としてのアイデンティティが強く意識されているようである。

Blanks to Fill in

Fill in the blanks with suitable words.

Christie Lu Stout (Anchor):

All week, we are live in front of Victoria Harbour as we approach the 20th anniversary of Hong Kong's handover to China. But this anniversary comes at a tense time as China tightens its grip on the city it now controls and activists grow bolder in their efforts to give the people of Hong Kong more power.

Christie Lu Stout (Reporter):

It's not easy being Hong Kong. It is simultaneously China and not China. It's a special administrative region, three words that distinguish it and Macao from the rest of the country.

To understand ⁽¹⁾_____ ⁽²⁾_____ ⁽³⁾_____ ⁽⁴⁾_____ ⁽⁵⁾_____, let's rewind more than 175 years, way back to 1841, when the British took control of Hong Kong from the Chinese during the First Opium War. Back then, it was just ⁽⁶⁾_____ ⁽⁷⁾_____ ⁽⁸⁾_____ ⁽⁹⁾_____ villages, but in more than a century under British rule, Hong Kong transformed into an international financial powerhouse.

The British introduced Western-style ⁽¹⁰⁾_____, ⁽¹¹⁾_____ ⁽¹²⁾_____ ⁽¹³⁾_____ ⁽¹⁴⁾_____ to Hong Kong. Hong Kongers also enjoyed freedom of expression and freedom of the press, liberties that don't exist in mainland China. As China was embroiled in international conflicts and civil war, Hong Kong thrived.

But in 1984, when Britain negotiated to give control of the territory back to China, people feared life would dramatically change. Under the "one country, two systems" principle, Beijing promised that Hong Kong would operate ⁽¹⁵⁾_____ ⁽¹⁶⁾_____ ⁽¹⁷⁾_____ ⁽¹⁸⁾_____ under British rule, for 50 years.

July 1st, 1997—the momentous return of Hong Kong from Britain to China. Since around the time of the handover, there has been constant soul-searching ⁽¹⁹⁾_____ ⁽²⁰⁾_____ ⁽²¹⁾_____ ⁽²²⁾_____ Hong Kong about their cultural identity, their political future and when this special administrative region would ⁽²³⁾_____ ⁽²⁴⁾_____ ⁽²⁵⁾_____ ⁽²⁶⁾_____ ⁽²⁷⁾_____ .

Critics say it's already started, pointing out China's refusal to grant Hong Kong free and fair elections for its top leader without Beijing vetting the candidates. And that sparked the Umbrella Movement protests that paralyzed the city's central business district (28)_____ (29)_____ (30)_____ (31)_____ (32)_____ in 2014.

Others will say life under Chinese rule has largely remained unchanged and that Hong Kong, Inc. has prospered along with the rise of China. Hong Kong still has an independent judiciary and a capitalist economy with its own financial system and currency.

But (33)_____ (34)_____ (35)_____ (36)_____ Beijing is increasingly imposing itself on the city's affairs. And then there's the question of what happens after China's promise of "one country, two systems" expires in 2047. Will Hong Kong be allowed to mostly run its own affairs, or be ruled just like any other Chinese city?

Twenty years after the handover, Hong Kong is proudly Hong Kong but divided between those who want more freedom and those who prefer not to mess with the motherland.

✏️ Notes

(Title) **neither one nor the other**「(二者のうちの) どちらでもない」

p. 95
(l. 2) **be live**「生放送している、実況中継している」　(l. 2) **Victoria Harbour**「ビクトリア・ハーバー」(香港の中心部にある湾・港)　(l. 3) **handover**「移譲、譲渡」　(l. 4) **tense**「緊迫した」　(l. 4) **tighten one's grip on ...**「～への支配力を強める」　(l. 5) **bold**「大胆な、勇敢な」　(l. 9) **special administrative region**「特別行政区」　(l. 9) **distinguish A from B**「B から A を際立たせる、A と B の違いを示す」(ここでは it and Macao が A に当たる)　(l. 10) **the rest of**「残りの」　(l. 12) **way back to ...**「ずっと昔の～へ」　(l. 13) **the First Opium War**「第一次アヘン戦争」　(l. 16) **powerhouse**「強力な組織・国」

p. 96
(l. 1) **introduce A to B**「A を B に導入する」　(l. 2) **Hong Konger**「香港人」　(l. 4) **be embroiled in ...**「(紛争などに) 巻き込まれる」　(l. 5) **civil war**「内戦、内乱」(中国国民党と中国共産党の国共内戦を指す。第 1 次 (1927～37年) と第 2 次 (1946年～49年) がある)　(l. 6) **negotiate to do**「～することを交渉して取り決める」　(l. 6) **give A back to B**「A を B に返還する」　(l. 8) **"one country, two systems" principle**「一国二制度」(中国本土は社会主義制度、香港は資本主義制度というように、一国の中に二つの制度の共存を認める方針)　(l. 8) **Beijing**「中国政府」　(l. 13) **soul-searching**「自己分析、内省」

p. 97
(l. 1) **grant A B**「A に B を許可する、認める」　(l. 2) **free and fair election**「自由で公正な選挙」　(l. 2) **vet**「(候補者などを) 綿密に調べる、審査する」　(l. 3) **candidate**「候補者」　(l. 3) **spark**「～を引き起こす、～の口火を切る」　(l. 3) **Umbrella Movement**「雨傘運動」(2014年に香港で起きた若者を中心とする大規模な民主化要求デモ)　(l. 4) **central business district**「中心業務地区」(市街地の中で、官庁・企業・商業施設などが集中する地区。略称 CBD)　(l. 6) **largely**「大部分は、主として」　(l. 7) **rise**「隆盛、台頭」　(l. 8) **judiciary**「司法制度」　(l. 8) **capitalist economy**「資本主義経済」　(l. 11) **impose oneself on ...**「～のことに出しゃばる」　(l. 11) **affairs**「事情、情勢、問題」　(l. 13) **be allowed to do**「～することを許される」　(l. 13) **run**「～を管理する、指揮する」　(l. 16) **(be) divided between A and B**「A と B に分かれる、分裂する」　(l. 16) **those who do**「～する人々」　(l. 16) **prefer not to do**「～することを望まない」　(l. 17) **mess with ...**「～との間にトラブルを起こす」　(l. 17) **the motherland**「母国、祖国」

Judgments to Make

[T / F] 1. Twenty years have passed since Hong Kong was given back to China by the British.

[T / F] 2. According to Christie Lu Stout, the statuses of Hong Kong and Macao are the same as that of the rest of China.

[T / F] 3. In 1841, Britain took control of Hong Kong.

[T / F] 4. Although Hong Kong is now an international financial powerhouse, it started as nothing more than a handful of fishing-villages.

[T / F] 5. During British rule, the people of Hong Kong had neither freedom of expression nor freedom of the press.

[T / F] 6. In 1984, when Britain decided to give control of Hong Kong back to China, Hong Kongers assumed that life would stay the same.

[T / F] 7. China refused to give Hong Kong free and fair elections for its position of top leader, without Beijing first evaluating the candidates.

[T / F] 8. Many people in Hong Kong are worried that the Chinese government is slowly gaining more and more control of the city's affairs.

 Partial Composition

1. デモ隊によって止められていた首都の水の供給を軍隊が掌握したとき、住民たちは安堵のため息をもらした。

   The residents heaved a sigh of relief as _____
   _____-supply, which had been disrupted by protestors.

2. 香港は自由社会であり、表現の自由と出版の自由を享受していると彼らは考えている。

   They think that Hong Kong is a free society and _____
   _____.

Unit 12

Giant Smog Trap

深刻な大気汚染に悩まされ続ける、北京をはじめとする中国の主要都市。そこに暮らす人々に健康被害をもたらす重大な問題でありながら、現状はなかなか改善されない。「何とかしなければ」と思い立った、あるオランダ人設計技師が新たな構想を打ち出した。各所に巨大な塔型の空気清浄機を設置し、その周囲の空気を浄化していこうというのだ。

 **Warm Up**

【聴き取りのポイント】

下線部に注意しながら、聴いてみよう。

 The tower is said to clean 30,000 cubic meters of air per hour.

> ポイント

下線部の数字や単位などに注意して聴いてみよう。

【内容理解のポイント】

次の文を考えてみよう。

Rapid industrialization has allowed blankets of pollution to cover the city below,

> ポイント

1. 下線部はどういう意味か考えてみよう。
2. 全体を訳してみよう。

Words and Phrases to Study

peer	inspire
laboratory	livable
particle	deter
radius	smog
synonymous	platform

Definition

deter   1. to discourage someone from doing something by scaring them with its possible negative consequences

_____   2. an opportunity to make progress in a particular area

_____   3. safe and comfortable for residents

_____   4. to give somebody an imaginative idea for something

_____   5. a room equipped with specialized equipment, and intended for scientific experiments, research, or the manufacture of chemicals

_____   6. an extremely small piece of matter that makes up some substance

_____   7. to look at something while concentrating because what is looked at is hard to see

_____   8. a specific area distant in all directions from a central point

_____   9. a fog or haze caused by pollutants released into the atmosphere

_____   10. so closely resembling something else that the two things seem to be the same

Examples

1. He was not in the slightest *deterred* by their rejection of his idea.

2. The word 'freedom' has become so closely tied to American culture that many consider it _____ with the phrase, 'the American way of life'.

3. The earthquake was sufficiently powerful for its shocks and tremors to be felt within a _____ of more than two hundred kilometers from its epicenter.

4. An invitation to give the opening speech at an international peace-conference provided the Princess of Wales with a perfect _____ from which to launch her campaign concerning land-mines.

5. Harry works at a _____ that develops new medicines designed to combat infectious diseases.

6. Cautiously, she opened the door only just enough for her to _____ into the dark room.

7. The design for Mercedes-Benz's newest model of car was _____ by the shape of the tropical box-fish.

8. What with its heat, its humidity, and the thousands of its foreign tourists, during summer this city is scarcely _____.

9. Do you think this tiny, bright thing could be a _____ of real gold?

10. When she left her apartment, the thickness of the _____ into which she walked prevented her from being able to see ahead for more than fifty meters.

中国やインドの大気汚染はアジア全域に影響を及ぼすほど深刻である。ことに中国では、大気汚染が原因で毎年100万人以上が死亡しているという。**PM2.5**が気になる北京をはじめ各大都市でも、天気予報とともに「深刻な大気汚染」というメッセージが出ることもしばしば。大気汚染の「赤色警報」**(Red Alert)** が出され、学校を閉鎖 **(shutting schools)**、数千台の車の道路への乗り入れ禁止 **(ordering thousands of vehicles off the roads)**、さらには住民への外出禁止 **(telling residents to stay indoors)** などの記事が新聞を賑わせる。1960年代後半から1970年代前半の日本の「公害」問題を想起させるが、規模の大きさからして問題はもっと深刻なようである。

Unit 12: Giant Smog Trap

Blanks to Fill in

Fill in the blanks with suitable words.

Andrew Stevens (Anchor):

A Dutch designer has come up with a new way to fight smog in one of the world's most heavily polluted cities, Beijing. He calls it the world's largest air purifier. Matt Rivers has more.

Matt Rivers (Reporter):

In Beijing, there are good days and ⁽¹⁾_____ ⁽²⁾_____ ⁽³⁾_____ ⁽⁴⁾_____. Unfortunately, these are the scenes that have become synonymous with the Chinese city. Rapid industrialization has allowed blankets of pollution to cover the city below, pushing it to its livable limits.

Daan Roosegaarde (Designer):

If you live in Beijing, it's the same as 17 cigarettes per day—⁽⁵⁾_____ ⁽⁶⁾_____ ⁽⁷⁾_____ ⁽⁸⁾_____ the nicotine. I mean: that…that is crazy. When did we say yes to that?

Matt Rivers:

It was just a few years ago when Dutch designer Daan Roosegaarde peered out [in]to a sea of smog from his window 32 stories up in Beijing and decided ⁽⁹⁾_____ ⁽¹⁰⁾_____ ⁽¹¹⁾_____ ⁽¹²⁾_____ .

Daan Roosegaarde:

We have designed the situation we are in, so we should also be able to design our way out of it.

Matt Rivers:

The design is a 7-meter-tall, smog-eating tower, which Roosegaarde describes as the world's largest air purifier.

Daan Roosegaarde:

And the design is actually inspired by the…by the Chinese temples, by the Chinese pagodas.

Matt Rivers:

The tower ⁽¹³⁾_____ ⁽¹⁴⁾_____ ⁽¹⁵⁾_____ ⁽¹⁶⁾_____ 30,000 cubic meters of air per hour. That's one football stadium per day. Using its ion technology, it collects and captures significant amounts of harmful airborne smog particles. The result is essentially a small radius of purified air surrounding the tower.

Daan Roosegaarde:

We have the scientific results to show that we can create parks which are 25 to 70 percent more clean than ⁽¹⁷⁾_____ ⁽¹⁸⁾_____ ⁽¹⁹⁾_____ ⁽²⁰⁾_____ ⁽²¹⁾_____, so that's really great. But at the same time, one tower will, of course, never…never solve the whole problem for the whole city.

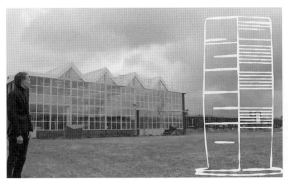

Matt Rivers:

Another study from the China Forum of Environmental Journalists actually found the tower is not as effective as claimed. But Roosegaarde has not been deterred from his mission.

Daan Roosegaarde:

There will always be people [who] say it's (22)_____ (23)_____ or it's (24)_____ (25)_____ or it (26)_____ (27)_____ (28)_____ or they already exist, or it's too fast or it's too slow or it's too beautiful, or it's too ugly or… You know, there are 5,000 reasons why we should *not* do things. I am interested in the five reasons (29)_____ (30)_____ (31)_____ (32)_____ (33)_____ .

Matt Rivers:

The tower has been making its way around China since last year, from Beijing to Tianjin to Dalian. Roosegaard sees this country as the perfect platform for this kind of innovation.

Daan Roosegaarde:

Some Chinese are (34)_____ (35)_____ (36)_____ (37)_____ (38)_____, but the conversation we had is: 'No, no, no, don't be ashamed. Every city is polluted, and London is more polluted five weeks ago than Beijing. You will be a laboratory for the future, for the smart city.'

Matt Rivers:

Matt Rivers, CNN, Beijing.

📝 Notes

p. 104
(l. 2) **come up with ...**「～を思いつく、考え出す」　　(l. 3) **heavily**「激しく、ひどく」　　(l. 3) **polluted**「汚染された」　　(l. 4) **air purifier**「空気清浄機」　　(l. 9) **push A to B**「AをBまで追い込む」　　(l. 14) **say yes to ...**「～を肯定する、受け入れる」　　(l. 17) **story**「(建物の) 階」

p. 105
(l. 3) **do one's way out of ...**「～することによって～ (という状況) から抜け出す」(doの部分にいろいろな動詞がくる)　　(l. 5) **-meter-tall**「高さ～メートルの」　　(l. 5) **-eating**「～を食べる」(ここでは「～を取り込んで除去する、なくす」という意味で使われている)　　(l. 6) **describe A as B**「AをBと表現する」　　(l. 9) **pagoda**「仏塔」　　(l. 12) **cubic meter**「立法メートル」　　(l. 13) **significant amounts of ...**「かなりの量の～、大量の～」　　(l. 14) **airborne**「空中に浮遊している」　　(l. 15) **purify**「～を浄化する、～から不純物を取り除く」

p. 106
(l. 2) **China Forum of Environmental Journalists**「中国環境新聞工作者協会」　　(l. 3) **find (that)**「(研究・調査などによって) ～という結論を出す」　　(l. 3) **claim (that) ...**「～だと主張する」　　(l. 13) **make one's way around ...**「～じゅうを動き回る、～のあちこちに進出する」　　(l. 14) **Tianjin**「天津」　　(l. 14) **Dalian**「大連」　　(l. 20) **smart city**「スマートシティー」(先端技術を用いて環境に配慮しながら、QOL (Quality of Live「生活の質」) を高めると同時に経済発展をめざす次世代都市のこと)

Judgments to Make

[T / F] 1. A Dutch designer has thought of an idea to help clean up Beijing's air, as Beijing is one of the most polluted cities in the world.

[T / F] 2. Rapid industrialization has helped to clean the air in Beijing.

[T / F] 3. According to Roosegaarde, living in Beijing is the same as smoking seventeen cigarettes a day.

[T / F] 4. Roosegaarde has designed a large device that he describes as 'the world's largest air purifier'.

[T / F] 5. The tower, inspired by Chinese pagodas, releases 30,000 cubic meters of harmful smog particles an hour.

[T / F] 6. Roosegaarde says that his invention can create parks which are up to seventy five percent cleaner than the rest of the city.

[T / F] 7. According to Roosegaarde, there are over 5,000 reasons for him to create his purifiers.

[T / F] 8. Roosegaarde's air purifier has been traveling around China for a year.

 Partial Composition

1. カリフォルニアの有名な果樹園やワイナリーの名前を聞けば、旅行客誰もが美味しい料理とお酒を思い浮かべます。

   The names of famous Californian vineyards and wineries have become _____ in the minds of every tourist.

2. 最近の研究によると、タミフルやリレンザのようなインフルエンザ薬は、言われるほど効能はないそうです。

   According to a recent research, flu medications such as Tamiflu and Relenza are _____ .

CNN: ビデオで見る世界のニュース (20)

検印 省略	©2019年1月31日 初版発行

編著者	関西大学 CNN 英語研究会
発行者	原　　雅　久
発行所	株式会社朝日出版社

101-0065　東京都千代田区西神田 3 - 3 - 5
電話（03）3239-0271
FAX（03）3239-0479
e-mail: text-e@asahipress.com
振替口座　00140-2-46008
組版・欧友社／製版・錦明印刷

乱丁，落丁本はお取り替えいたします
ISBN978-4-255-15632-3 C1082